AMAZING BIBLE PUZZLES

New Testament

Nancy I. Sanders

Concordia Publishing House
St. Louis

For Dan

Scripture quotations are taken from the HOLY BIBLE, NEW INTERNATIONAL VERSION®. Copyright © 1973, 1978, 1984 by the International Bible Society. Used by permission of Zondervan Publishing House. All rights reserved.

The "NIV" and "New International Version" trademarks are registered in the United States Patent and Trademark Office by the International Bible Society. Use of either trademark requires the permission of the International Bible Society.

Copyright © 1993 Concordia Publishing House
3558 S. Jefferson Avenue, St. Louis, MO 63118-3968
Manufactured in the United States of America

Teachers may reproduce pages for classroom use only.

All rights reserved. Except as noted above, no part of this publication may be reproduced, stored in a retrieval system, or transmitted, in any form or by any means, electronic, mechanical, photocopying, recording, or otherwise, without the prior written permission of Concordia Publishing House.

1 2 3 4 5 6 7 8 9 10   02 01 00 99 98 97 96 95 94 93

A BABY ANNOUNCEMENT   JESUS' BIRTH
                        Luke 2:1-20

Use the underlined words in this story to fill in the blank puzzle. Be careful to put each word in the correct boxes so that all the words will fit. One word has already been written in the puzzle.

"And there were <u>shepherds</u> living out in the fields nearby, keeping watch over their flocks at <u>night</u>. An angel of the Lord appeared to them, and the glory of the Lord <u>shone</u> around them, and they were terrified. But the <u>angel</u> said to them, 'Do not be afraid. I bring you good <u>news</u> of great <u>joy</u> that will be for all the people. Today in the town of David a <u>Savior</u> has been born to you; he is <u>Christ</u> the Lord. This will be a sign to you: You will find a <u>baby</u> wrapped in cloths and lying in a <u>manger</u>' "(Luke 2:8-12 NIV).

© 1993 CPH

FALLING STARS   THE MAGI
                        Matthew 2:1-12

   The magi followed a special star. This star led them
to the special child, Jesus. When the magi traveled through
Jerusalem, a certain king heard about them. This king
secretly planned to kill Jesus.
   Follow the paths of these falling stars. Only five
stars fall the whole way to the ground. Trace the paths to
find out which ones fall to the bottom. Write their letters
in the blank stars below. You will find out the name of the
king.

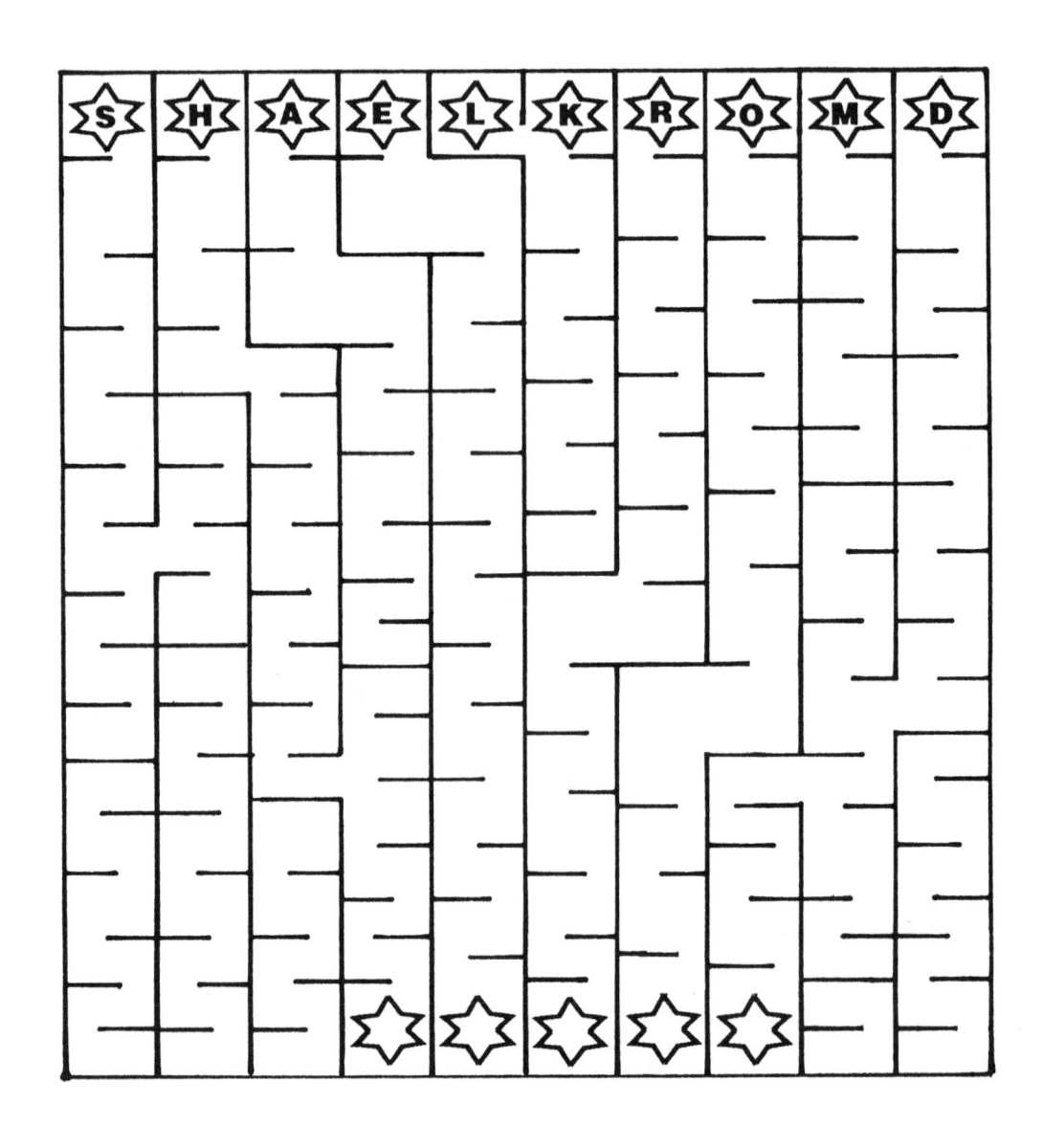

4   © 1993 CPH

LOST AND FOUND   JESUS LOST AT THE TEMPLE
                       Luke 2:41-50

When Jesus was 12, his family went to Jerusalem for the Feast of Passover. On the way home, Jesus' parents discovered he was missing. Help Mary and Joseph find Jesus in the temple courts in Jerusalem.

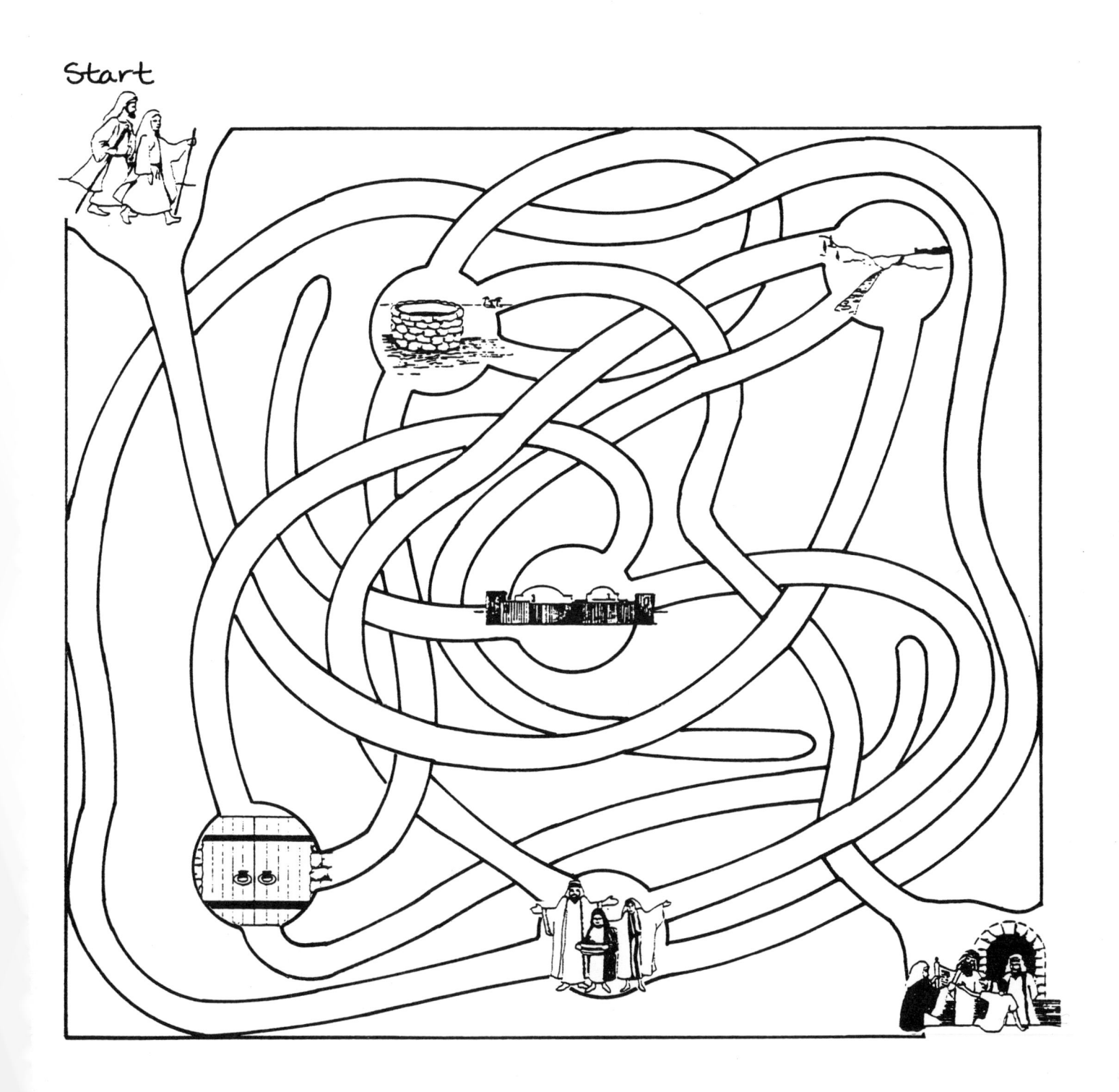

Start

© 1993 CPH

5

TIME TO GET WET   JOHN THE BAPTIST
                         Luke 3:3

John the Baptist baptized people in the Jordan River. He taught people to be sorry for the wrong things they had done.

Using this code, write the letters on the blanks. You will see why John wanted people to be baptized.

CODE:

A	B	C	D	E	F	G	H	I
J	K	L	M	N	O	P	Q	R
S	T	U	V	W	X	Y	Z

ANSWER:

F M R

F M R G I V E N E S S

M F J H E I R

S I N S

DID YOU HEAR THAT?   JESUS' BAPTISM
                      Luke 3:21-22

   When John baptized Jesus, heaven opened. The Holy
Spirit came down on Jesus in the shape of a dove. A voice
from heaven spoke.
   Beginning at the arrow, write down every other word.
Go around the dove twice. Then you can read what the
heavenly voice said to Jesus.

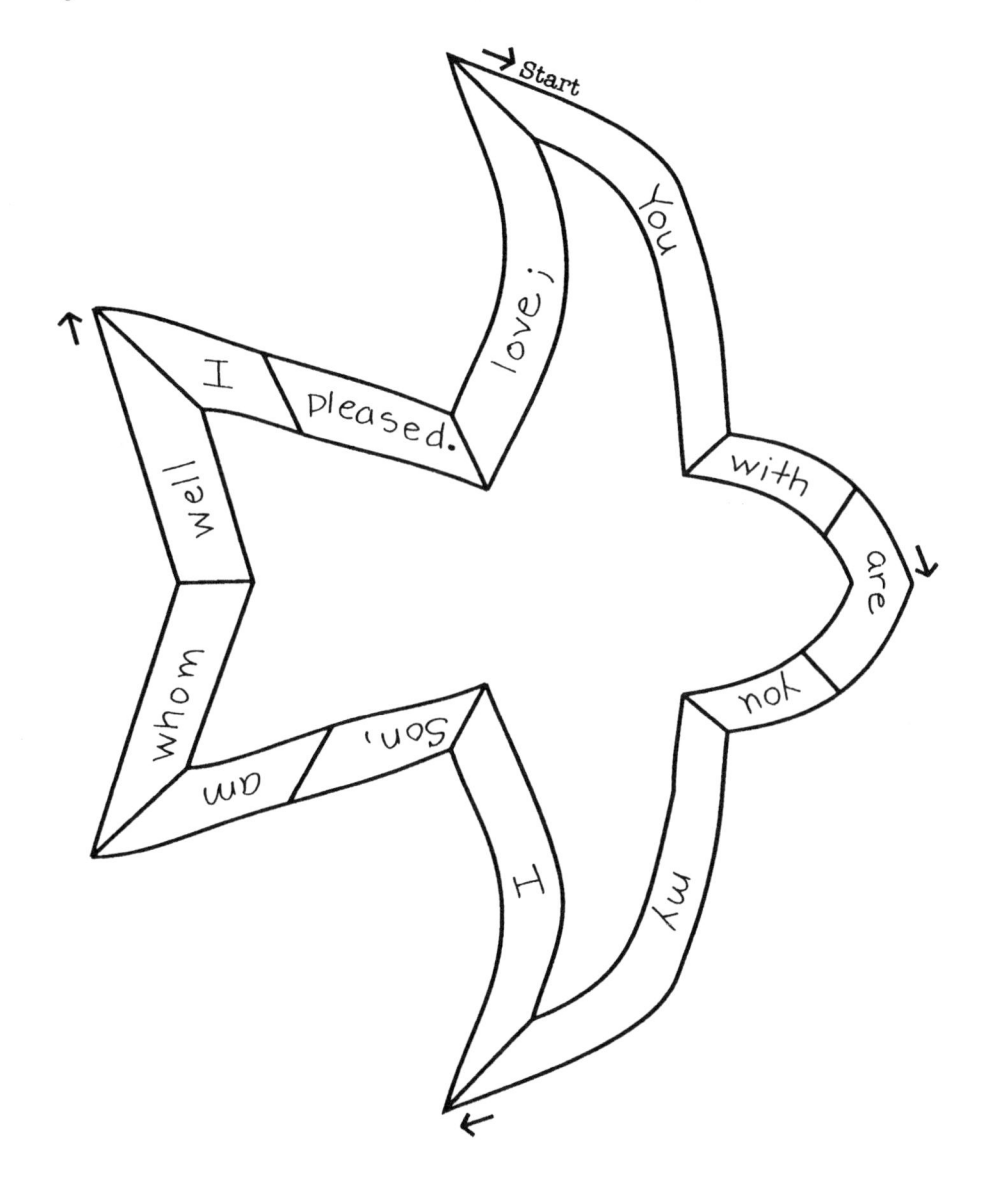

_____
_____
_____

(Luke 3:22 NIV)

© 1993 CPH   7

A TEMPTING TIME   THE TEMPTATION OF JESUS
                         Luke 4:1-13 NIV

Fill in this crossword puzzle about the temptation of Jesus. Use the words in the word list if you need help.

ACROSS
3. The devil said to Jesus, "If you are the Son of God, tell this stone to become _____."
5. Jesus answered, "It is _____: 'Man does not live on bread alone.'"
7. The devil led Jesus to a high place and showed him all the kingdoms of the world. And he said to him, "I will give you all their _____ and splendor."
9. The devil said to Jesus, "So if you _____ me, it will all be yours."
10. Jesus _____, "It is written: 'Worship the Lord your God and serve him only.'"

DOWN
1. The devil had Jesus stand on the highest point of the _____.
2. The devil said, "If you are the Son of God, _____ yourself down from here."
4. "Because," said the devil, "it is written: 'He will command his angels to guard you and _____ you up in their hands so you will not strike your foot against a stone.'"
6. Jesus answered, "It says: 'Do _____ put the Lord your God to the test.'"
8. When the devil had finished all this _____, he left Jesus until another time.

WORD LIST:
ANSWERED
AUTHORITY
BREAD
LIFT
NOT
TEMPLE
TEMPTING
THROW
WORSHIP
WRITTEN

GONE FISHING   **JESUS CALLS HIS DISCIPLES**
                    Mark 1:16-20

There are four fish caught in this net. Each fish has a disciple's name written on it in code. The letter written in the fish is the letter of the alphabet which comes before the actual letter of the correct name. Figure out the correct names which belong on the fish. You will then know who the first four disciples were.

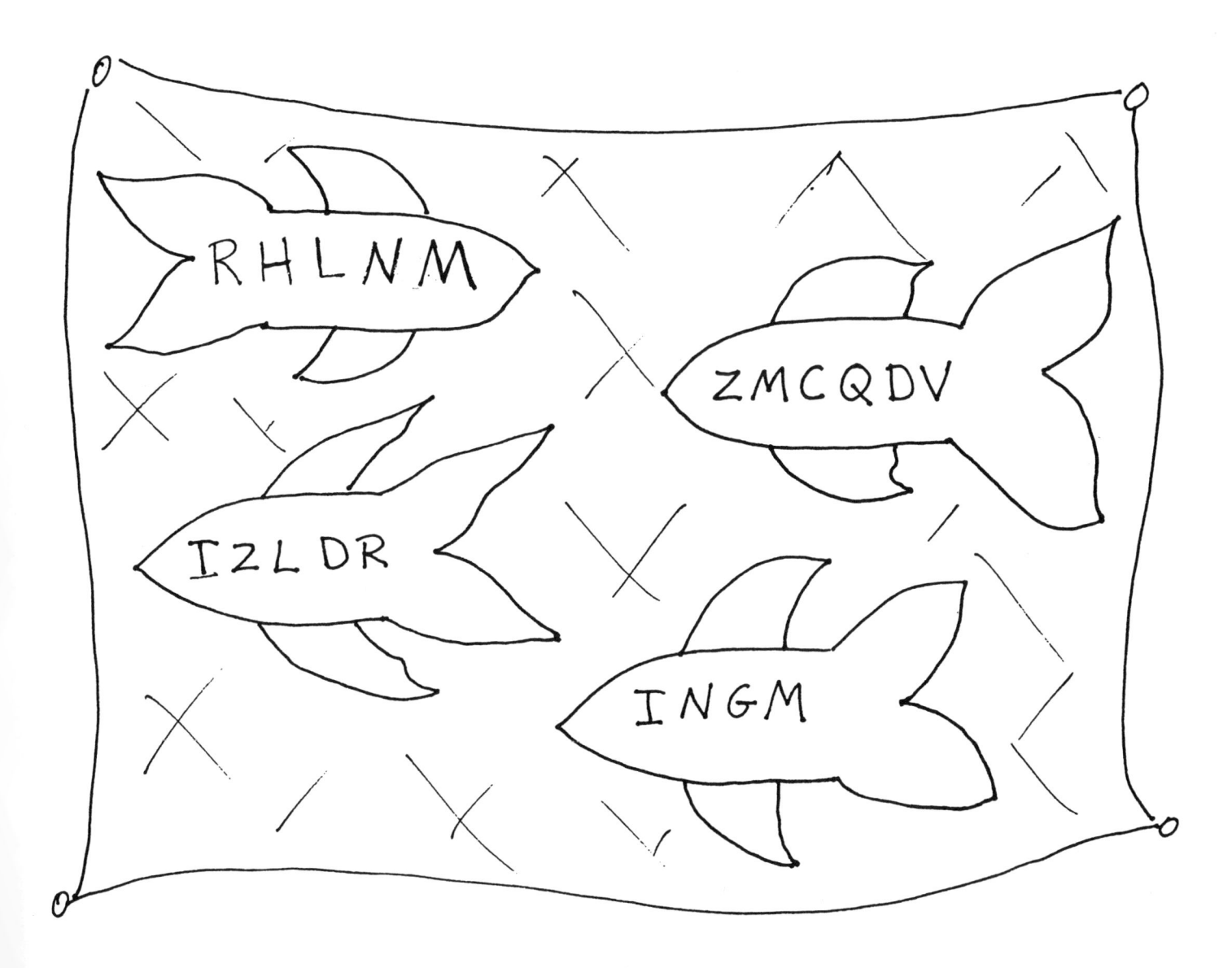

- RHLNM
- ZMCQDV
- IZLDR
- INGM

© 1993 CPH

ALONE　　　　　　　　　　JESUS WITHDREW FROM THE CROWDS
　　　　　　　　　　　　　　Luke 5:16

   Crowds of people followed Jesus everywhere. He taught
them and healed the sick. But often Jesus went away from
everyone to be alone. To find out what Jesus did when he
was alone, write down the first letter of each item,
beginning with 1.
         Jesus __ __ __ __ __ __.
               1 2 3 4 5 6

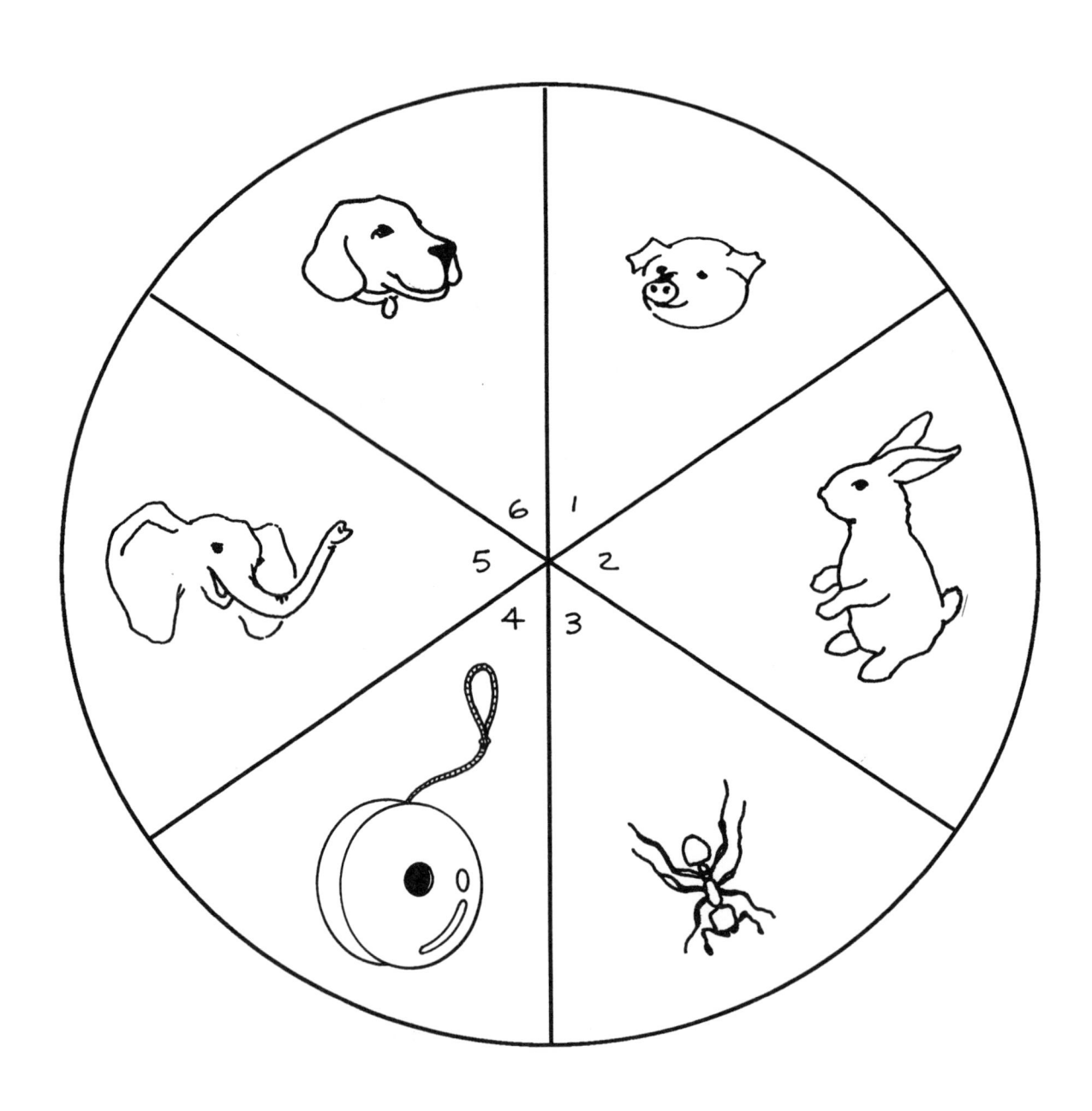

10   © 1993 CPH

HEAL ME! THE PARALYTIC
Luke 5:17-26

A man was paralyzed. He could not walk. His friends carried him on a mat to see Jesus. When they got to the house, there were many people! It was too crowded, and they could not get close to Jesus.

Starting at the top, go down this list of letters and cross out all the X's. Return to the top. Going down, write the words on the blanks. You will see how the man got close to Jesus so that he could be healed.

```
X
H
E
X
W
E
N
T
X
D
O
W
N
X
T
H
R
O
U
G
H
X
T
H
E
X
R
O
-
O
F
X
```

_____
_____

A PARTY

LEVI'S BANQUET
Luke 5:27-32

A tax collector named Levi gave a great banquet for Jesus. When the Pharisees saw this, they asked Jesus, "Why do you eat with these sinners?"

Using this code, look across the picture column and down the number column to write the correct letters above the blanks. You will know the answer Jesus gave to the Pharisees.

CODE	1	2	3	4	5
○	T	W	A	B	N
△	R	I	H	L	C
□	H	U	S	T	E
◇	Y	E	D	O	K

$\overline{\triangle 2}\ \overline{\bigcirc 1}\quad \overline{\triangle 2}\ \overline{\square 3}\ \overline{\bigcirc 5}\ \overline{\diamond 4}\ \overline{\square 4}\quad \overline{\bigcirc 1}\ \overline{\triangle 3}\ \overline{\diamond 2}$

$\overline{\square 1}\ \overline{\diamond 2}\ \overline{\bigcirc 3}\ \overline{\triangle 4}\ \overline{\bigcirc 1}\ \overline{\triangle 3}\ \overline{\diamond 1}\quad \overline{\bigcirc 2}\ \overline{\triangle 3}\ \overline{\diamond 4}$

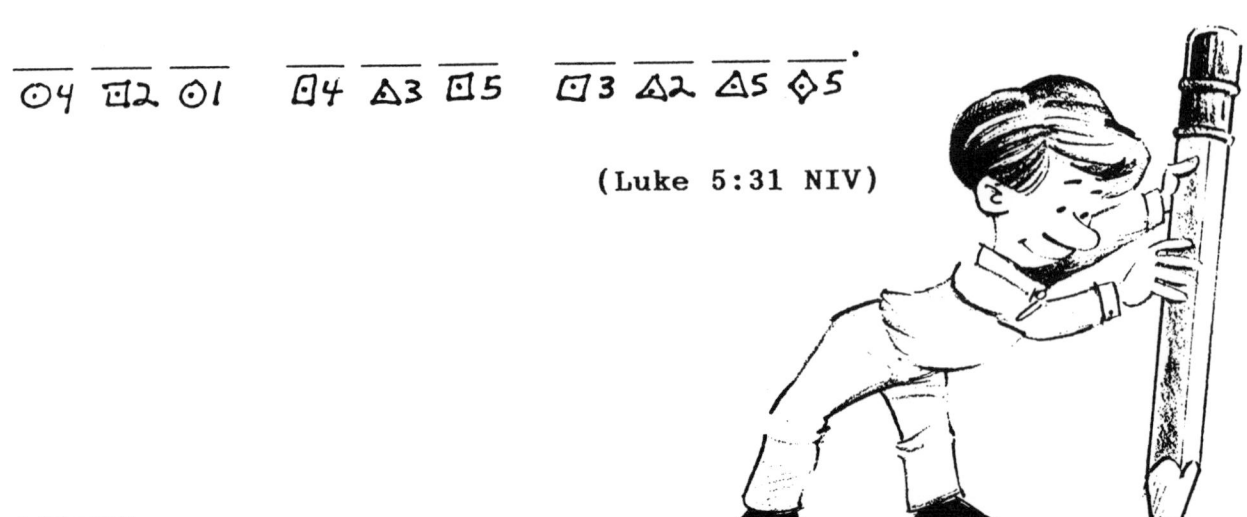

$\overline{\bigcirc 5}\ \overline{\square 5}\ \overline{\diamond 2}\ \overline{\diamond 3}\quad \overline{\bigcirc 3}\quad \overline{\diamond 3}\ \overline{\diamond 4}\ \overline{\triangle 5}\ \overline{\square 4}\ \overline{\diamond 4}\ \overline{\triangle 1}$,

$\overline{\bigcirc 4}\ \overline{\square 2}\ \overline{\bigcirc 1}\quad \overline{\square 4}\ \overline{\triangle 3}\ \overline{\square 5}\quad \overline{\square 3}\ \overline{\triangle 2}\ \overline{\triangle 5}\ \overline{\diamond 5}$.

(Luke 5:31 NIV)

12   © 1993 CPH

PICK A NUMBER   CHOOSING DISCIPLES
                     Luke 6:12-13

One night Jesus went to a mountainside to pray. In the morning he chose his disciples. How many disciples did he pick? To find out, follow the path. Add the numbers, writing the answers in the blanks. When you reach the end you will know how many disciples Jesus chose.

Start

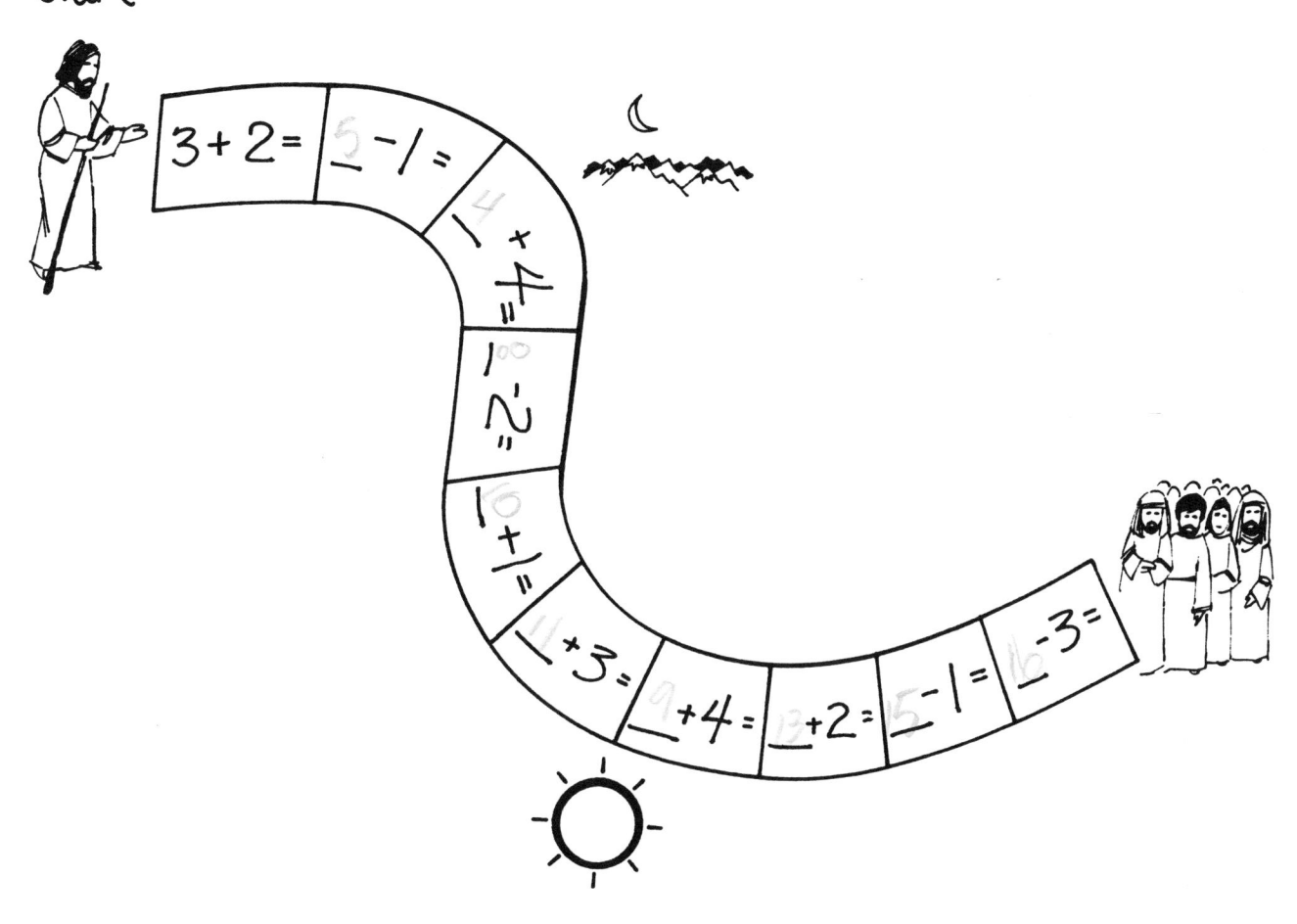

3+2= 5-1= 4+4= 8-2= 6+1= 7+3= 10+4= 14+2= 16-1= 15-3=

© 1993 CPH

ENEMIES! SERMON ON THE MOUNT
Matthew 5:44

During the Sermon on the Mount, Jesus taught the people many things. One lesson was about love. To find out what Jesus said about love, fill in the boxes with these letters:

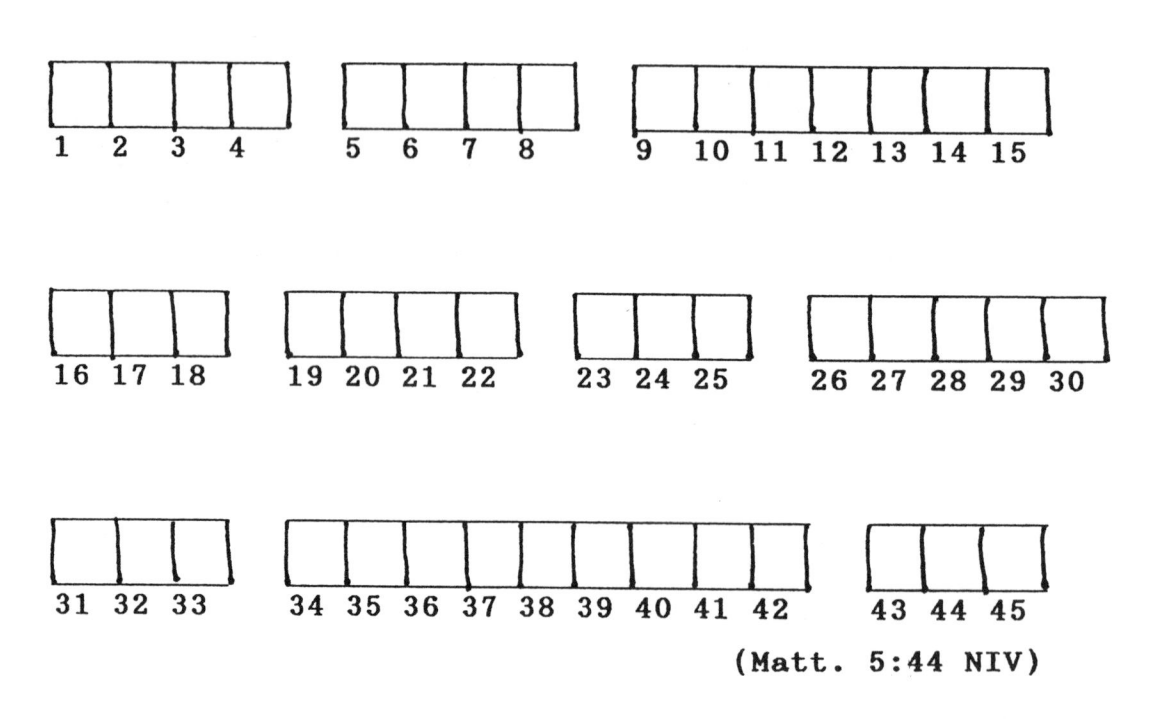

A- BOXES 16,21
C- BOX 39
D- BOX 18
E- BOXES 4,9,11 14,30,35,38,42
F- BOX 23
H- BOXES 27,32

I- BOX 13
L- BOX 1
M- BOX 12
N- BOXES 10,17
O- BOXES 2,6,24 28,33,44
P- BOXES 19,34

R- BOXES 8,20,25,36
S- BOXES 15,29,37
T- BOXES 26,41
U- BOXES 7,40,45
V- BOX 3
W- BOX 31
Y- BOXES 5,22,43

(Matt. 5:44 NIV)

© 1993 CPH

SPECIAL LOVE   JESUS IS ANOINTED
                     Luke 7:36-50

A sinful woman came into the house where Jesus was eating. She anointed him with expensive perfume. Jesus forgave her sins.

To see exactly how she anointed Jesus, trace the lines from top to bottom to complete the sentences.

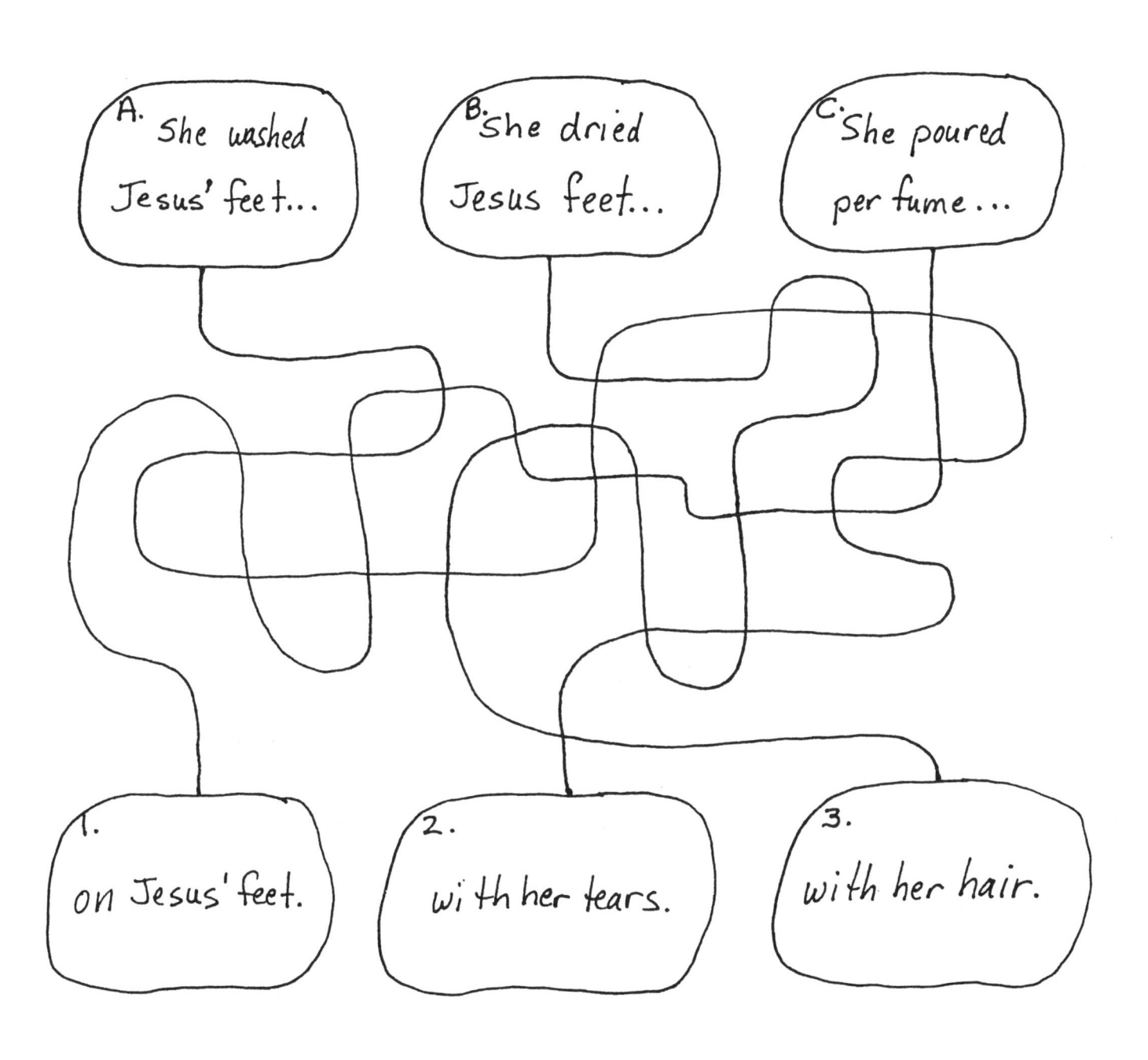

A. She washed Jesus' feet...

B. She dried Jesus feet...

C. She poured perfume...

1. on Jesus' feet.

2. with her tears.

3. with her hair.

© 1993 CPH   15

STORY TIME   THE PARABLE OF THE SOWER
                    Luke 8:4-8, 11-15

A parable is a story that has a special meaning. Fill in
the vowels to read this parable that Jesus told.

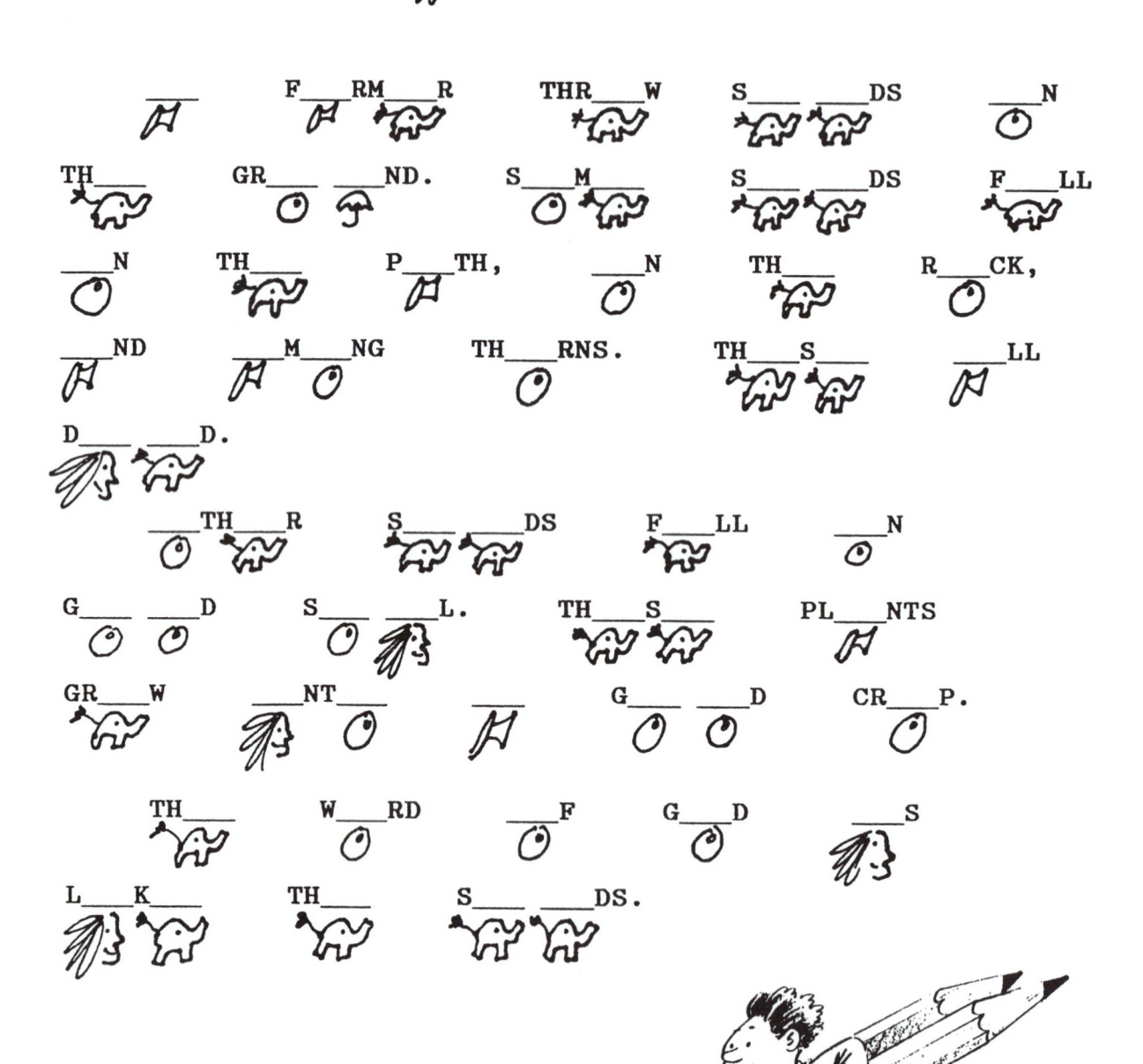

VOWELS: A   E   I   O   U

A F_RM_R THR_W S__DS _N
TH_ GR__ND. S_M_ S__DS F_LL
_N TH_ P_TH, _N TH_ R_CK,
_ND _M_NG TH_RNS. TH_S_ _LL
D__D.

_TH_R S__DS F_LL _N
G__D S__L. TH_S_ PL_NTS
GR_W _NT_ A G__D CR_P.

TH_ W_RD _F G_D _S
L_K_ TH_ S__DS.

16   © 1993 CPH

STORMY WEATHER **JESUS CALMS THE STORM**
Luke 8:22-25

One day Jesus slept in the boat as the disciples sailed across the lake. A sudden storm fell on them. They were in great danger! The disciples woke Jesus to ask for help.
Jesus got up and spoke to the storm. To find out what happened, color in the squares which contain the following numbers. Then read the words found in the rest of the spaces.

Color in these spaces:
4,10,11,12,20,21,25,26,27,31,32,33,39,40,45,46

1 T	2 H	3 E	4 Z	5 S	6 T	7 O	8 R	9 M	10 Y
11 B	12 W	13 S	14 T	15 O	16 P	17 P	18 E	19 D	20 E
21 A	22 A	23 N	24 D	25 O	26 X	27 J	28 T	29 H	30 E
31 J	32 L	33 P	34 W	35 A	36 T	37 E	38 R	39 H	40 I
41 G	42 R	43 E	44 W	45 N	46 L	47 C	48 A	49 L	50 M.

© 1993 CPH   17

DON'T PACK A SUITCASE   SENDING OUT THE 12
                            Luke 9:1-6

   Jesus sent his 12 disciples out to visit the villages. He told them to stay as guests at people's homes. While there, they would preach the Gospel and heal the sick.
   Look at the translating chart below. Using this chart, translate the following words into English. You will discover the list of things Jesus told the disciples NOT to take on their journey.

TRANSLATING CHART

ARLP--journey   QUAVI--for
BOLGA--the   SHO--no
DALTE--money   SHOLENTA--nothing
KRECKLE--staff   WALPE--bread
MECKLE--Take   YALPA--tunic
MEEZA--extra   ZIGGLE--bag

TRANSLATE THESE WORDS:

MECKLE   SHOLENTA   QUAVI   BOLGA   ARLP-

SHO   KRECKLE,   SHO   ZIGGLE,   SHO   WALPE,

SHO   DALTE,   SHO   MEEZA   YALPA.

_____
_____
_____

                              (Luke 9:3 NIV)

18   © 1993 CPH

WE'RE HUNGRY!   **FEEDING THE 5,000**
                    Matthew 14:13-21

A large crowd followed Jesus. As evening came, they were hungry. Jesus did a miracle and fed all of them!
Circle the word that doesn't belong in each slice of bread. Write the words, in order, on the following lines. You will see what Jesus used to feed 5,000 people.

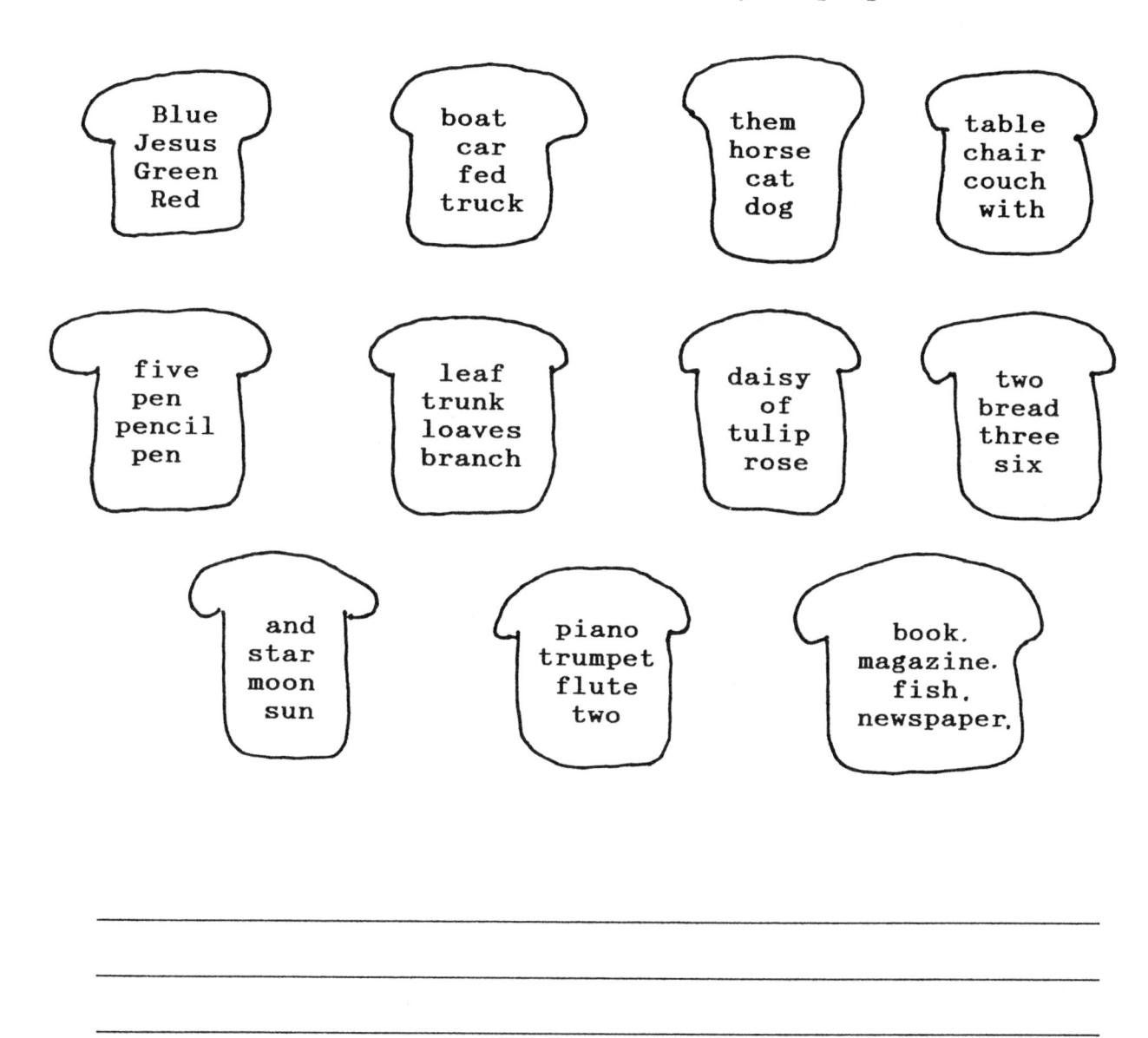

- Blue / **Jesus** / Green / Red
- boat / car / **fed** / truck
- **them** / horse / cat / dog
- table / chair / couch / **with**
- **five** / pen / pencil / pen
- leaf / trunk / **loaves** / branch
- daisy / **of** / tulip / rose
- **two** / bread / three / six
- **and** / star / moon / sun
- piano / trumpet / flute / **two**
- book / magazine / **fish** / newspaper

_____
_____
_____

© 1993 CPH   19

WHO AM I?   PETER'S CONFESSION
Luke 9:18-20

The crowds thought Jesus was Elijah or some other prophet. One day Jesus asked the disciples, "Who do you say I am?"

To see what Peter answered, look at the pictures. Write the first letter of each word in the box. Then read the words.

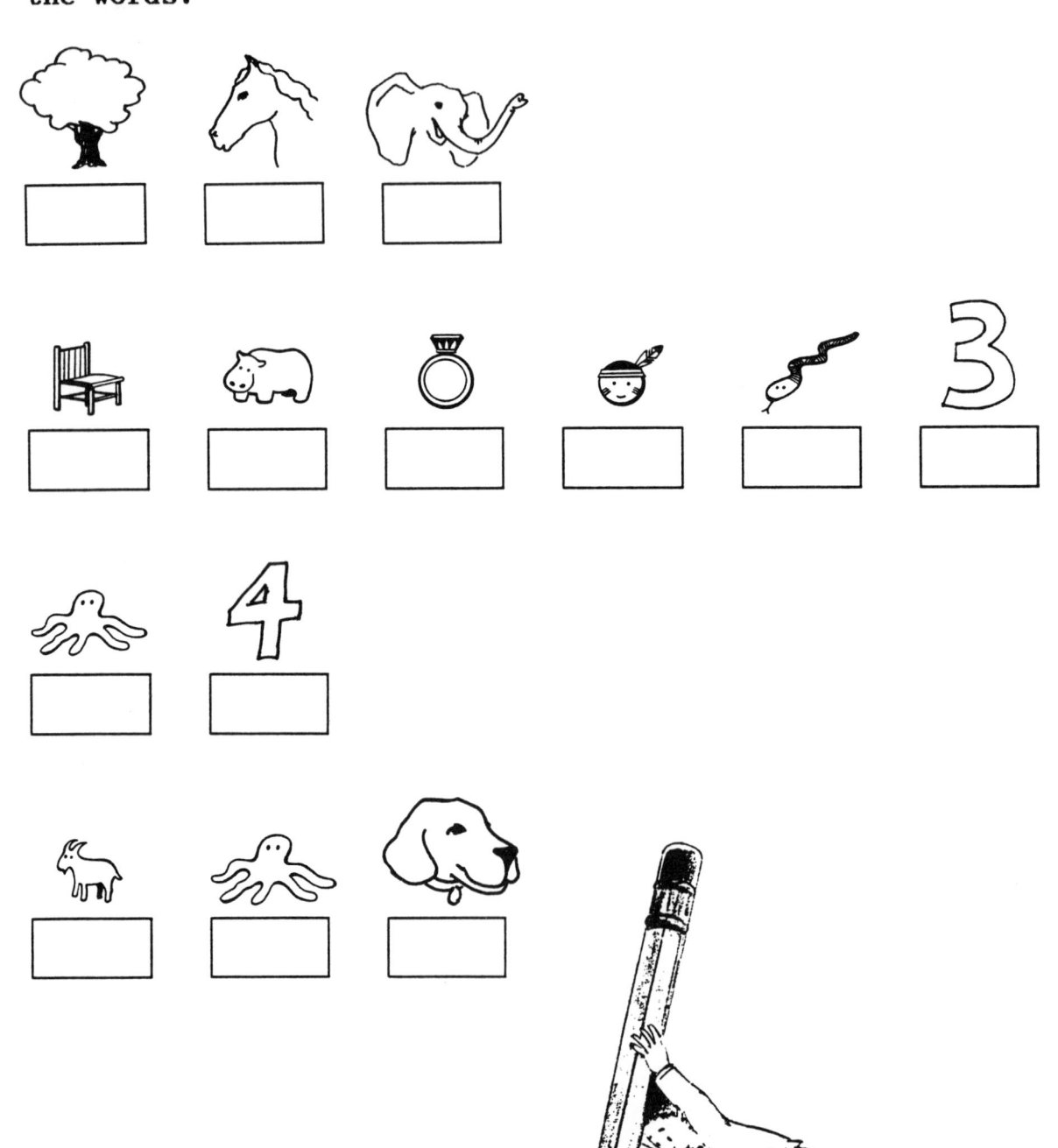

20 © 1993 CPH

THE VOICE

JESUS SPEAKS WITH MOSES AND ELIJAH
Luke 9:28-36

Peter, John, and James went with Jesus to a mountain to pray. As Jesus prayed, Moses and Elijah appeared and talked with him. Then a voice spoke from a cloud.

Using the following code, figure out the words which were spoken from the cloud. This is Morse Code, a code used to send messages over the telegraph.

[Morse code chart A–Z]

[Coded message] (Luke 9:35 NIV)

ROAD SIGNS   THE GOOD SAMARITAN
                          Luke 10:25-37

   Printed on these signs are the words which fit in the
blanks of this story. Each sign was broken in half. Can
you match the signs to form the words to complete this
story?

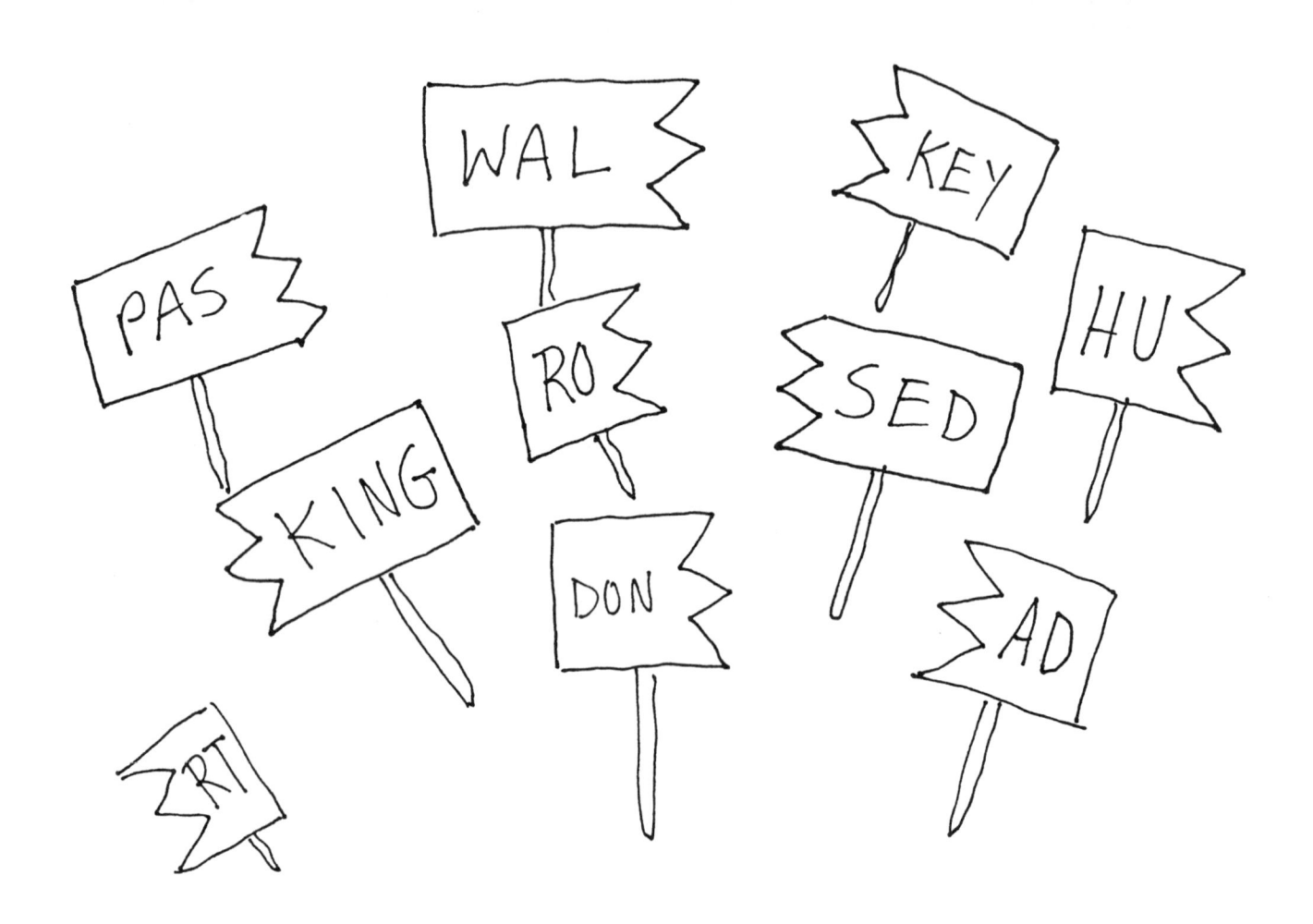

[Signs: PAS, WAL, KEY, KING, RO, SED, HU, DON, AD, RT]

   A man was going to Jericho. Robbers beat him and left
him lying in the _____. A priest came _____
down the road. When he saw the hurt man, he passed by on
the other side of the road. A Levite came along the road.
He _____ by on the other side, too. A Samaritan also
came along. When he saw the _____ man, he stopped and
helped him. He put the man on his _____ and took him to
an inn until he got well.

HOW? JESUS TEACHES HOW TO PRAY
Luke 11:1-4

Read the following clues. Write the answers in the matching horizontal boxes. Then take the letters found in the numbered boxes and write them down to complete this sentence:

These words are commonly called
"The Lord's __ __ __ __ __ __".
           1 2 3 4 5 6

CLUES:

One of the 1._____ said to Jesus, "Lord, teach us to pray."
Jesus answered, "When you 2._____, say:
'Father,
hallowed be your 3._____,
your kingdom come.
Give us each 4._____
our daily 5._____.
Forgive us our sins,
for we also 6._____ everyone
who sins against us.
And lead us not into temptation.'" (Luke 11:2-4 NIV)

WORD LIST:
BREAD
DAY
DISCIPLES
FORGIVE
NAME
PRAY

© 1993 CPH
23

I FOUND IT!   THE LOST SHEEP
              Luke 15:4-7

Jesus told the parable of the lost sheep. When the shepherd found the sheep, he called everyone to rejoice with him. Jesus explained that there also is much rejoicing in heaven when one sinner repents.
Help the shepherd find the lost sheep.

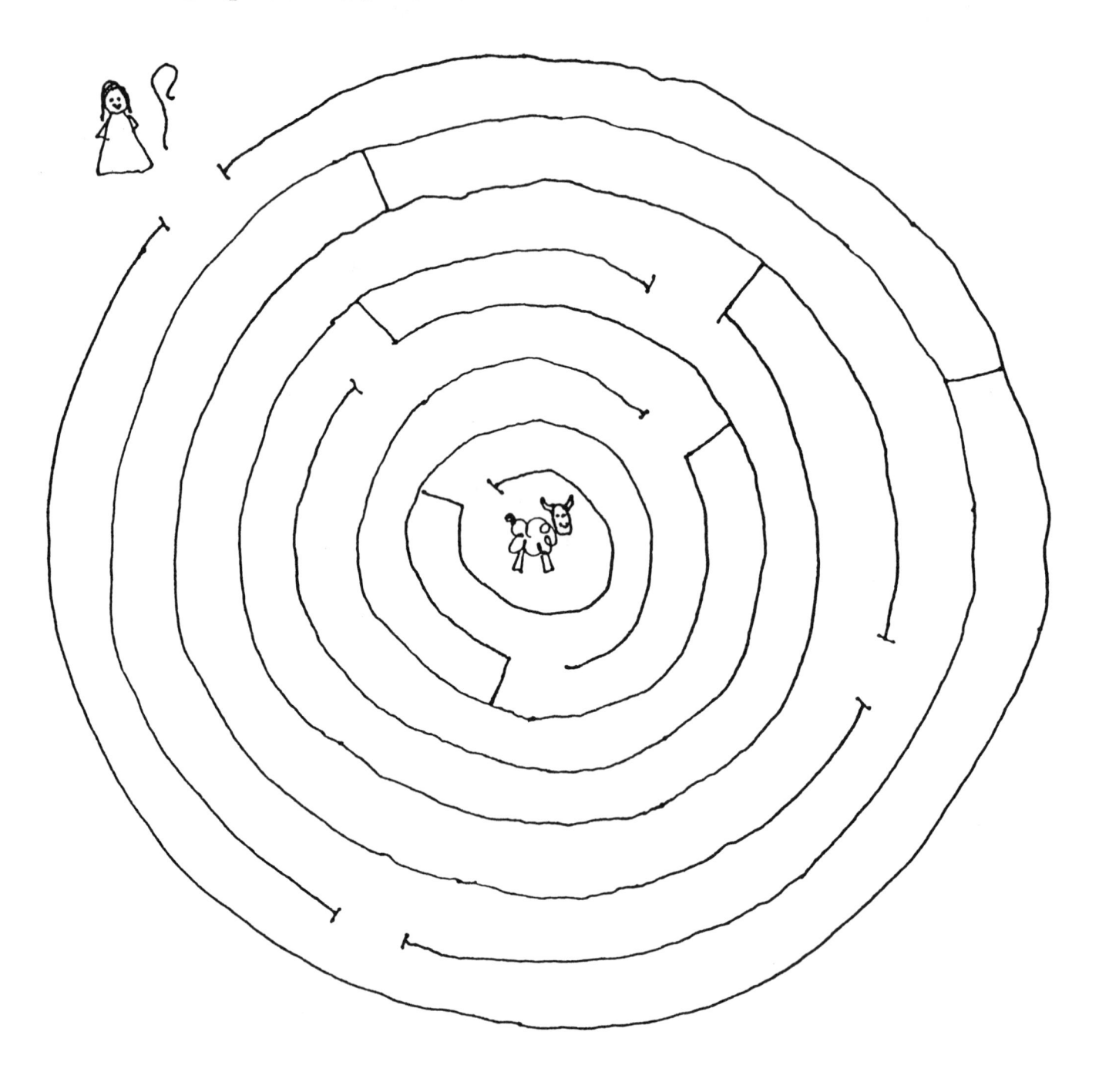

HOME AGAIN   THE PRODIGAL SON
                          Luke 15:11-32

Jesus told a parable about a father and his two sons. He explained how one son left home and did many wrong things. When the son came back to ask for forgiveness, the father was very glad. To see what the father said when the son came home, unscramble these words:

YM   OSN   AWS   SOLT

TUB   ONW   SI   OUNDF.

_____

_____

_____

© 1993 CPH

25

GO AWAY? JESUS AND THE CHILDREN
Matthew 19:13-15

People brought their little children to Jesus so that he could hold them. When the disciples saw this, they told the people to go away.
Use this code to fill in the letters above the blanks. You will find out what Jesus said about this situation.

```
CODE
A-1     H-8     O-15    U-21
B-2     I-9     P-16    V-22
C-3     J-10    Q-17    W-23
D-4     K-11    R-18    X-24
E-5     L-12    S-19    Y-25
F-6     M-13    T-20    Z-26
G-7     N-14
```

$\overline{10}\ \overline{5}\ \overline{19}\ \overline{21}\ \overline{19}$ $\overline{19}\ \overline{1}\ \overline{9}\ \overline{4}$,

"$\overline{12}\ \overline{5}\ \overline{20}$ $\overline{20}\ \overline{8}\ \overline{5}$ $\overline{12}\ \overline{9}\ \overline{20}\ \overline{20}\ \overline{12}\ \overline{5}$

$\overline{3}\ \overline{8}\ \overline{9}\ \overline{12}\ \overline{4}\ \overline{18}\ \overline{5}\ \overline{14}$ $\overline{3}\ \overline{15}\ \overline{13}\ \overline{5}$

$\overline{20}\ \overline{15}$ $\overline{13}\ \overline{5}$." (Matt. 19:14 NIV)

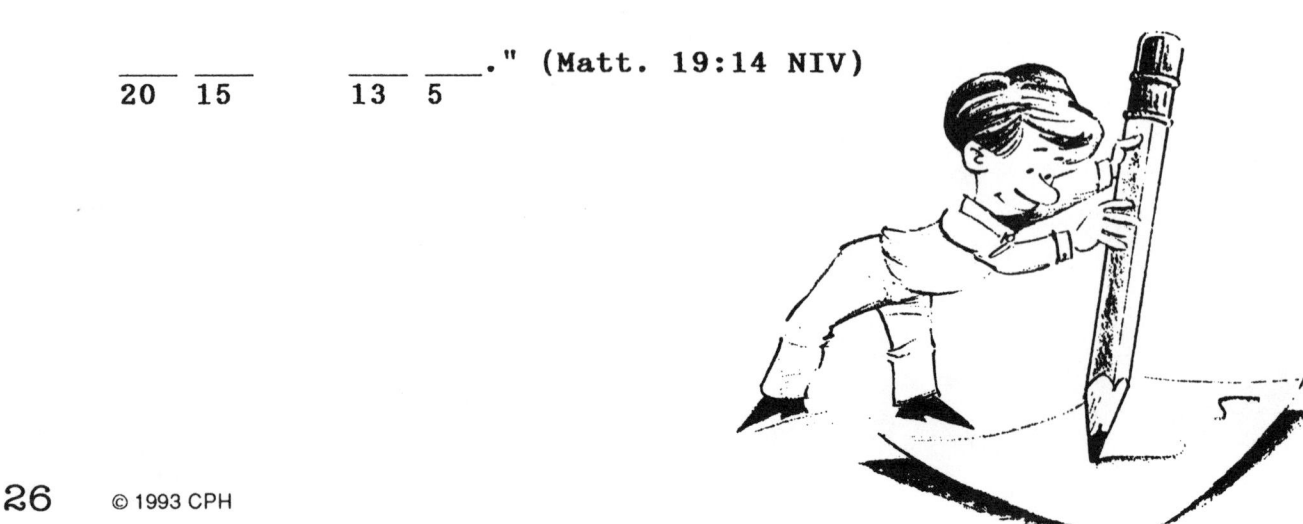

© 1993 CPH

COME DOWN, ZACCHAEUS!

ZACCHAEUS
Luke 19:1-10

Use the underlined words in this story to fill in the blank puzzle. Be careful to put each word in the correct boxes so that all the words will fit. One word has already been written in the puzzle.

Jesus traveled through <u>Jericho</u>. A short man named Zacchaeus wanted to see him. Zacchaeus was a <u>tax</u> collector who <u>cheated</u> and took people's money. There was such a big <u>crowd</u> that Zacchaeus climbed a <u>tree</u> and looked down. When Jesus walked by, he stopped under the tree. "Come <u>down</u>, Zacchaeus!" said Jesus. "I must <u>stay</u> at your house today!"

<u>Zacchaeus</u> climbed down and was happy to meet Jesus. "<u>Look</u>, Lord!" he said. "Today I will pay back anyone I cheated."

Jesus said, "Today salvation has come to this <u>house</u>."

© 1993 CPH

27

PRAISE THE LORD! TRIUMPHAL ENTRY
John 12:12-15

Jesus was going to Jerusalem for the Passover. He rode a donkey into the city. People joyfully waved palm branches and shouted words of praise.

Using this code, look across the picture column and down the number column to write the correct letters above the blanks. You will see what the people said to praise Jesus.

CODE	1	2	3	4
♛	D	F	O	C
✝	S	N	A	W
☼	I	T	L	H
♥	B	E	R	M

HOSANNA! BLESSED

IS   HE   WHO   COMES

IN   THE   NAME

OF   THE   LORD!

(John 12:13 NIV)

A FINAL MEAL   THE PASSOVER
                    Luke 22:7-23; John 13:1-17

   Jesus ate the Passover meal with his disciples. This was the final time he ate with them before he died. During this meal, he washed the disciples' feet and taught them many things about his love for them.
   In this puzzle are three different kinds of letters. Write down the letters beside the numbers that match them. Next, unscramble each matching set of letters to find out what we commonly call this important meal.

1. _____

2. _____

3. _____

THE KISS   BETRAYAL IN THE GARDEN
                    Mark 14:43-46

When the soldiers entered the Garden of Gethsemane to arrest Jesus, they knew who he was because one of the disciples kissed him.
To find out which disciple betrayed Jesus with a kiss, write down the first letter of each word, beginning with 1.

__ __ __ __ __
 1   2 3 4 5

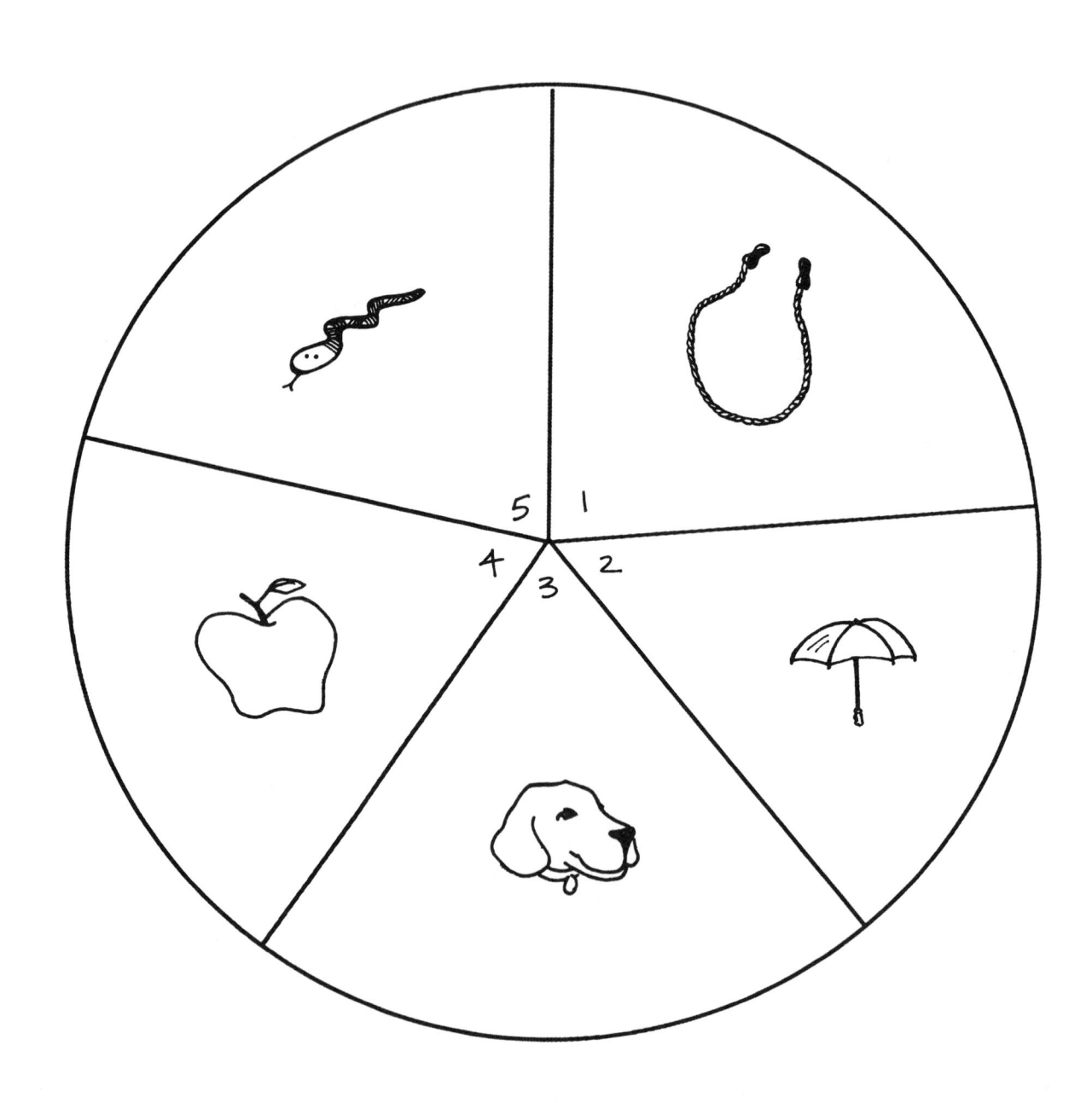

TRUE LOVE   JESUS' DEATH ON THE CROSS
                         Luke 23:32-46

   Jesus died on the cross for our sins because he loves each one of us so much. His love was shown even as he felt pain on the cross.
   To find out the words of love that Jesus spoke for the people who crucified him, fill in the boxes with these letters:

A-2,36,42   M-17
D-25,45   N-27,31,48
E-5,13,16,23,40,44   O-8,19,26,28,32,46
F-1,7,18   R-6,9,20,43
G-10,49   T-3,14,21,29,37,38
H-4,15,22,35,39   V-12
I-11,47   W-33,34
K-30   Y-24,41

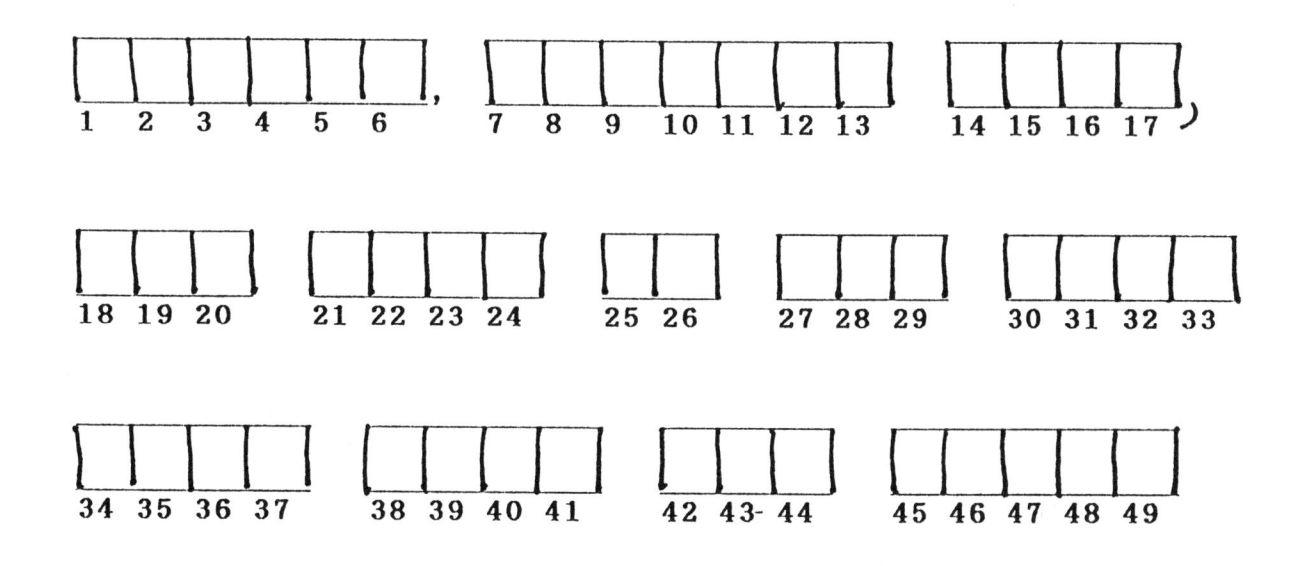

□□□□□□ , □□□□□□□ □□□□)
1 2 3 4 5 6   7 8 9 10 11 12 13   14 15 16 17

□□□ □□□□ □□ □□□ □□□□
18 19 20   21 22 23 24   25 26   27 28 29   30 31 32 33

□□□□ □□□□ □□□ □□□□□
34 35 36 37   38 39 40 41   42 43 44   45 46 47 48 49

(Luke 23:34 NIV)

© 1993 CPH   31

WHERE IS HE? **THE RESURRECTION**
Luke 24:1-12

On the third day after Jesus died, the women visited his tomb. Suddenly two men with shining clothes stood before them.

Beginning at the arrow, write down every other word. Go around the picture of the empty tomb twice. Then you can read what the special men said.

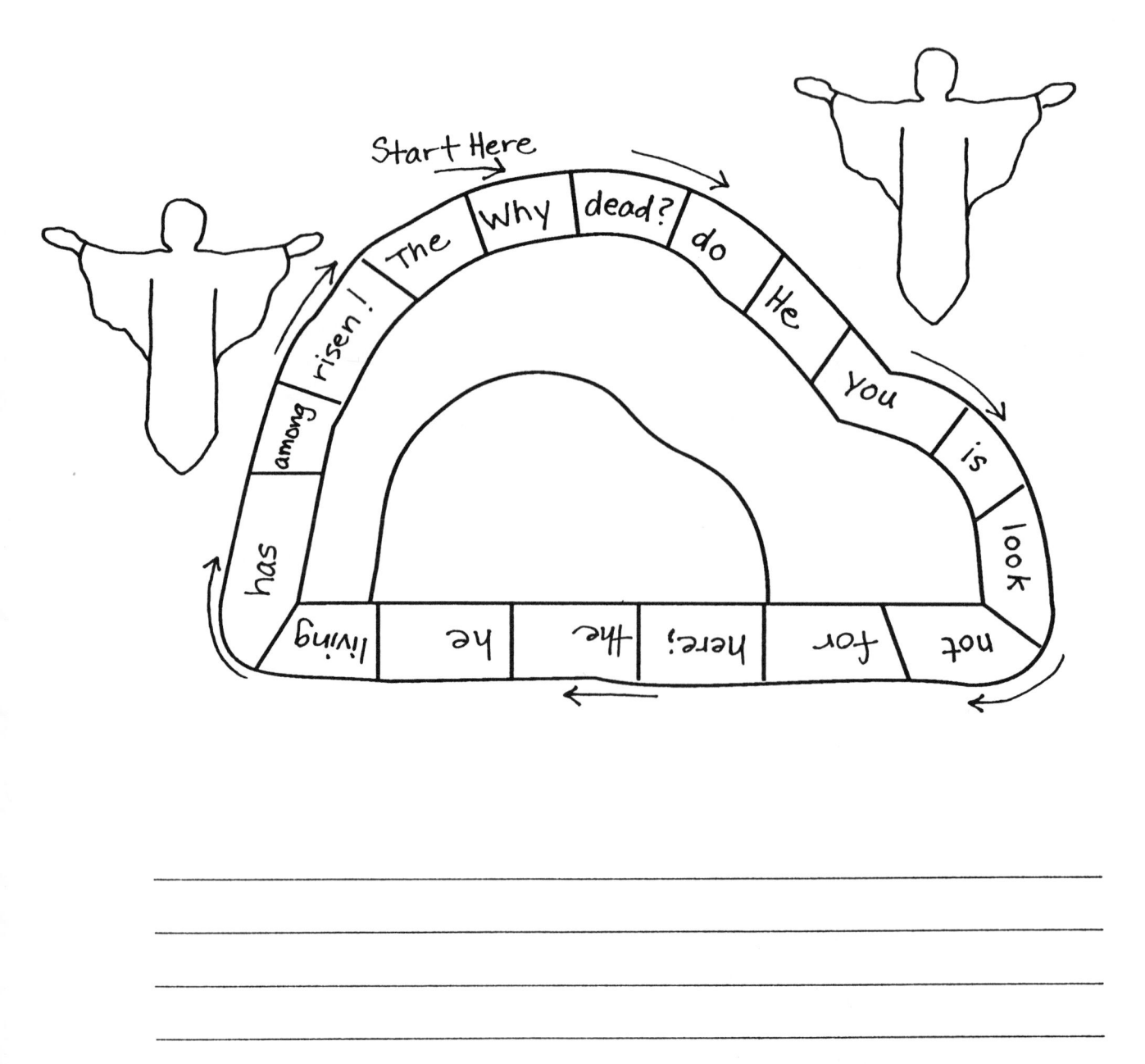

Start Here: The Why dead? do He you is look not for here; the he living has among risen! The

_____
_____
_____
_____

(Luke 24:5-6 NIV)

32 © 1993 CPH

I DOUBT IT! THE DISCIPLE WHO DID NOT BELIEVE
John 20:24-29

After Jesus rose from the dead, he visited many of the disciples. One disciple had not seen him yet. This doubting disciple said, "I will not believe Jesus is alive unless I can touch the nail scars on his hands." Jesus soon appeared and let the disciple touch him so that he would believe.

Follow the paths of these letters as they drop through the maze. Only six letters fall the whole way down. Trace the paths to find out which ones fall to the bottom. Write these letters in the circles below. You will find out the name of this disciple.

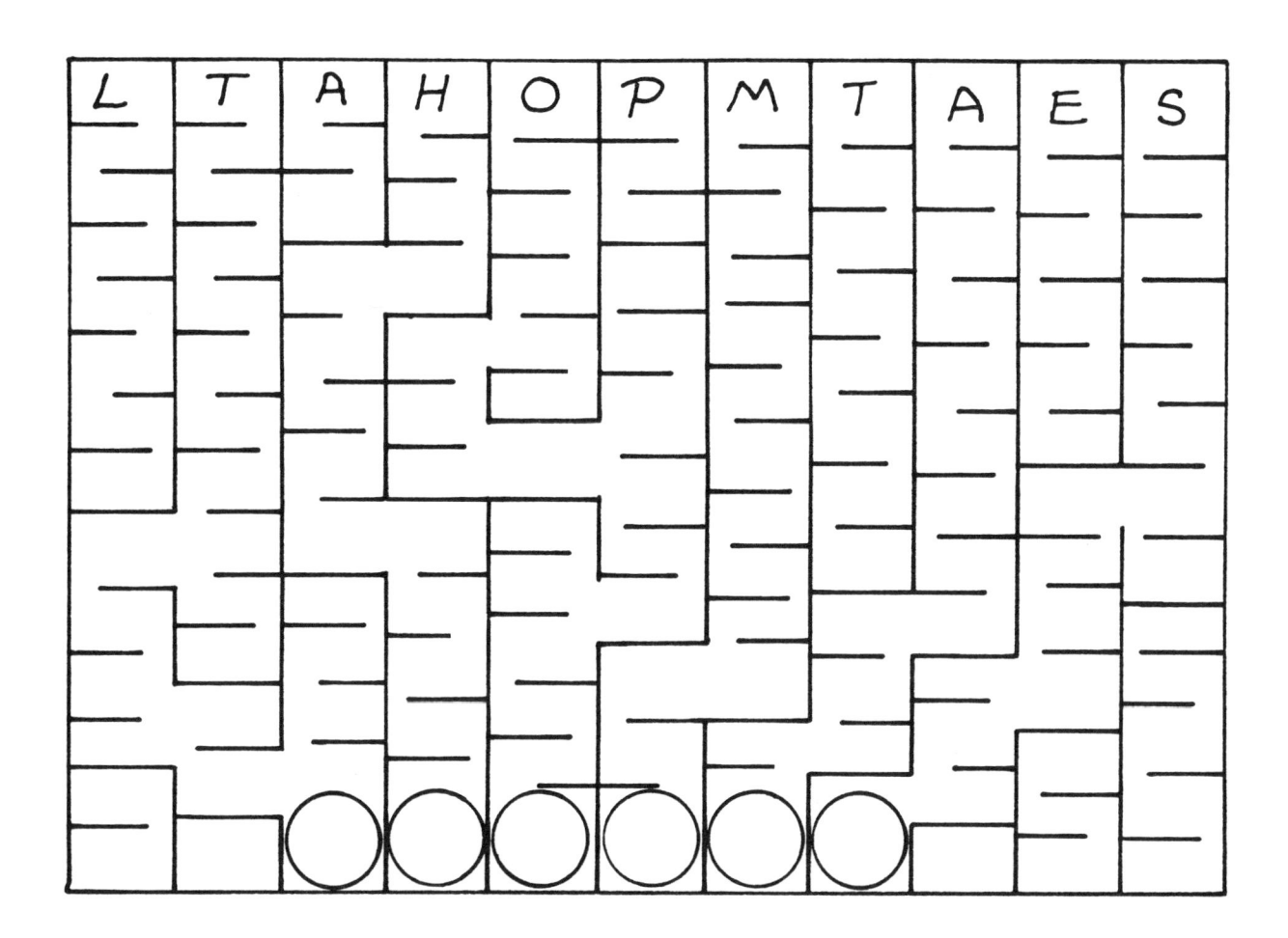

L T A H O P M T A E S

UP, UP, AND AWAY   THE ASCENSION
                        Acts 1:9-11

   After Jesus rose from the dead, he appeared to the disciples for 40 days. Then he went back to heaven.
   Circle the word that doesn't belong in each cloud. Write the words, in order, on the lines below. You will see how Jesus went to heaven.

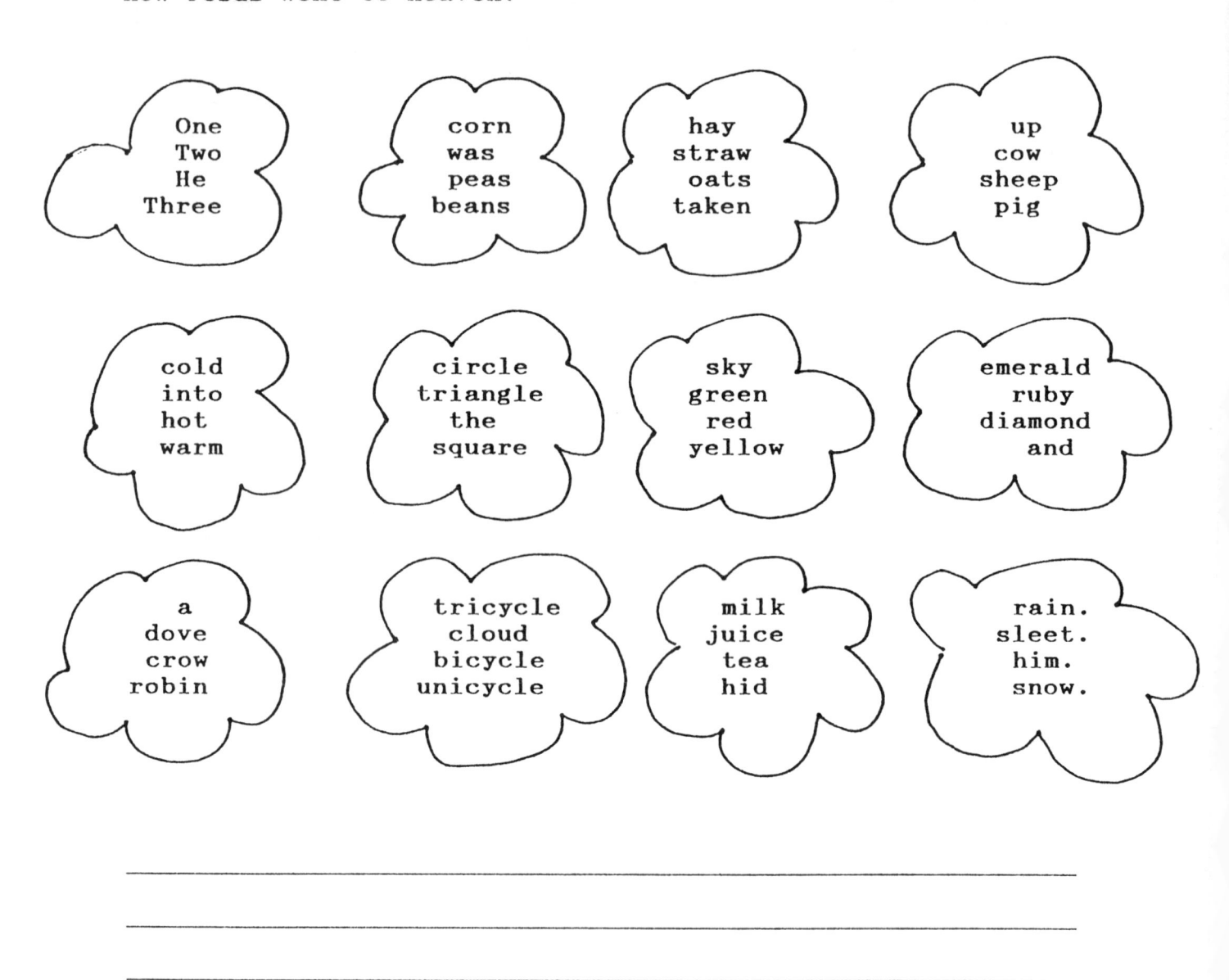

Cloud 1	Cloud 2	Cloud 3	Cloud 4
One / Two / He / Three	corn / was / peas / beans	hay / straw / oats / taken	up / cow / sheep / pig
cold / into / hot / warm	circle / triangle / the / square	sky / green / red / yellow	emerald / ruby / diamond / and
a / dove / crow / robin	tricycle / cloud / bicycle / unicycle	milk / juice / tea / hid	rain. / sleet. / him. / snow.

_____

_____

_____

34   © 1993 CPH

A WONDERFUL, WONDER-FILLED DAY   PENTECOST
                                  Acts 2:1-4

The day of Pentecost came, and the early believers were all together in one place. A sound like a roaring wind filled the house, and tongues of fire came to rest above each person.
Look at the translating chart below. Using this chart, translate the following words into English. You will see what else happened on this wonder-filled day of Pentecost.

TRANSLATING CHART:

AWNTO-HOLY   KOOGLE-ALL
BOLP-OTHER   LEGGLE-THE
CHORTLEX-WITH   MARKA-THEM
DARUGA-LANGUAGES   NEZ-IN
GELPA-SPIRIT   RERRE-FILLED
HEMK-AND   SQUOLT-SPOKE
JIDDO-WERE   ZEE-OF

TRANSLATE THESE WORDS:

   KOOGLE   ZEE   MARKA   JIDDO   RERRE

   CHORTLEX   LEGGLE   AWNTO   GELPA   HEMK

   SQUOLT   NEZ   BOLP   DARUGA.

_____

_____

_____

© 1993 CPH   35

WALK! PETER HEALS THE LAME MAN
Acts 3:1-8

Fill in the vowels to read this story.

VOWELS: A E I O U

ONE DAY, PETER AND JOHN
WERE GOING TO THE TEMPLE. A
CRIPPLED MAN STOPPED THEM AND
ASKED FOR MONEY. PETER SAID,
"SILVER OR GOLD I DO NOT
HAVE, BUT WHAT I HAVE I
GIVE YOU. IN THE NAME OF
JESUS, WALK!" THE MAN JUMPED TO
HIS FEET AND BEGAN TO WALK!
HE PRAISED GOD FOR THIS MIRACLE.

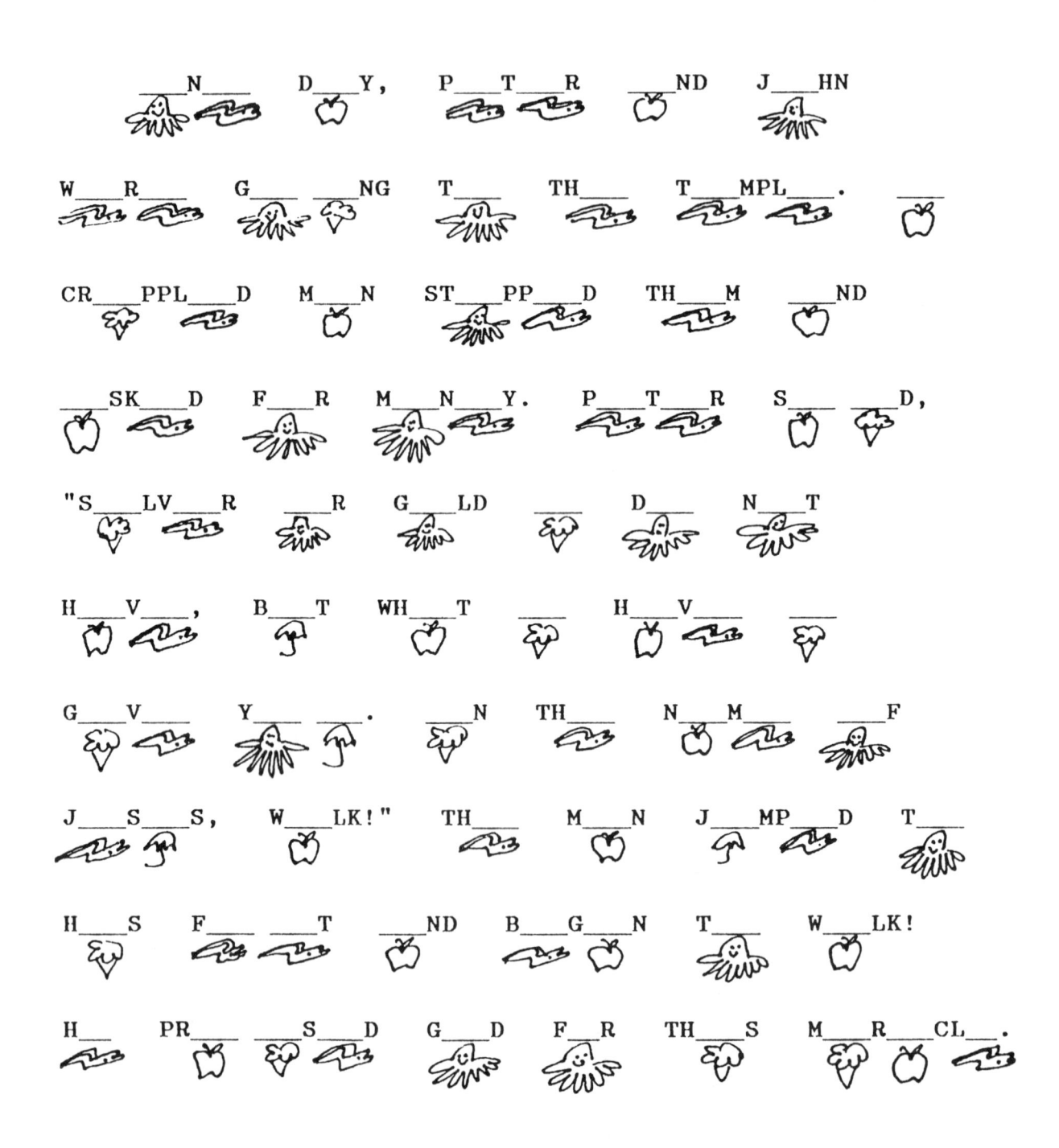

36 © 1993 CPH

THIS NEWS IS GOOD NEWS   PHILIP AND THE ETHIOPIAN
                           Acts 8:26-39

An angel told Philip to go down a desert road. On his walk, Philip met an Ethiopian riding in a chariot. Philip and the Ethiopian talked. After hearing Philip's message, the Ethiopian asked to be baptized.

To see what Philip told the Ethiopian, color in the squares which contain the following numbers. Then read the words found in the rest of the spaces.

Color in these squares: 1,2,9,10,15,16,20,21,22,26, 31,36,37,38,39,40,41,42,43,49,50,51,57,58,59,60.

1 X	2 B	3 P	4 H	5 I	6 L	7 I	8 P	9 E	10 A
11 T	12 O	13 L	14 D	15 J	16 N	17 H	18 I	19 M	20 O
21 M	22 C	23 T	24 H	25 E	26 Y	27 G	28 O	29 O	30 D
31 W	32 N	33 E	34 W	35 S	36 Z	37 U	38 Q	39 E	40 H
41 D	42 V	43 F	44 A	45 B	46 O	47 U	48 T	49 U	50 R
51 S	52 J	53 E	54 S	55 V	56 S	57 B	58 D	59 E	60 A

© 1993 CPH

WHO TURNED ON THE LIGHT? **THE ROAD TO DAMASCUS**
Acts 9:1-19 NIV

Complete the crossword puzzle. Use the word list if you want.

ACROSS
3. A man named Saul tried to kill the new _____.
6. When he was on the road to Damascus, a light _____ around him.
7. Saul fell to the ground and heard a _____.
10. The voice said, "Saul, Saul, why do you _____ me?"
11. "_____ are you, Lord?" Saul asked.
12. "I am _____, whom you are persecuting," said the voice.

DOWN
1. Saul stood up, but when he opened his _____, he saw nothing.
2. They led Saul to the city, where he _____.
4. After three days, a man placed his hands on _____, and he could see again.
5. Saul now believed in Jesus and was _____.
8. Later, Saul's name was changed to _____.
9. Paul spread the good news about Jesus _____ he went.

WORD LIST:
BAPTIZED
CHRISTIANS
EVERYWHERE
EYES
FLASHED
JESUS
PAUL
PERSECUTE
PRAYED
SAUL
VOICE
WHO

WHAT'S FOR DINNER? PETER'S VISION
Acts 10:9-20

One day Peter saw a vision. In the vision, a sheet came down from heaven. The sheet held many animals. God had told his people not to eat these animals. God told Peter he could eat them. Through this experience and the things that happened next, Peter learned that he could share the good news of Jesus with people who weren't Jews.

Try to find some of these animals which Peter might have seen in his vision. Their names can go up, down, backward, forward, or diagonally.

ALLIGATOR	HERON
BAT	OWL
CAMEL	PIG
CHAMELEON	RABBIT
EAGLE	RAVEN
GULL	STORK
HAWK	VULTURE

```
Z C H A M E L E O N
L J W L X B E N E O
P L Q L O H M V Y R
I A U I W N A D M E
G O X G L R C W P H
E L G A E J Y X K C
V U L T U R E G N B
W S T O R K Q H R A
S L X R A B B I T T
```

© 1993 CPH 39

KNOCK, KNOCK, WHO'S THERE?

PETER ESCAPES FROM PRISON
Acts 12:1-19

Peter was arrested and chained in prison. One night, an angel came to the prison and set Peter free! The angel led Peter out of the prison gate. Then Peter went to a friend's house to tell what happened. When he knocked at the door, the servant girl was so excited that she forgot to open the door and let Peter in the house! Instead, she ran to tell everyone that Peter was free. Peter was left standing outside the door.

Answer each math question to help Peter get to his friend's house. Then, using the chart, write the matching letter above each answer. Put the letters together in this new order to spell the name of the forgetful servant girl.

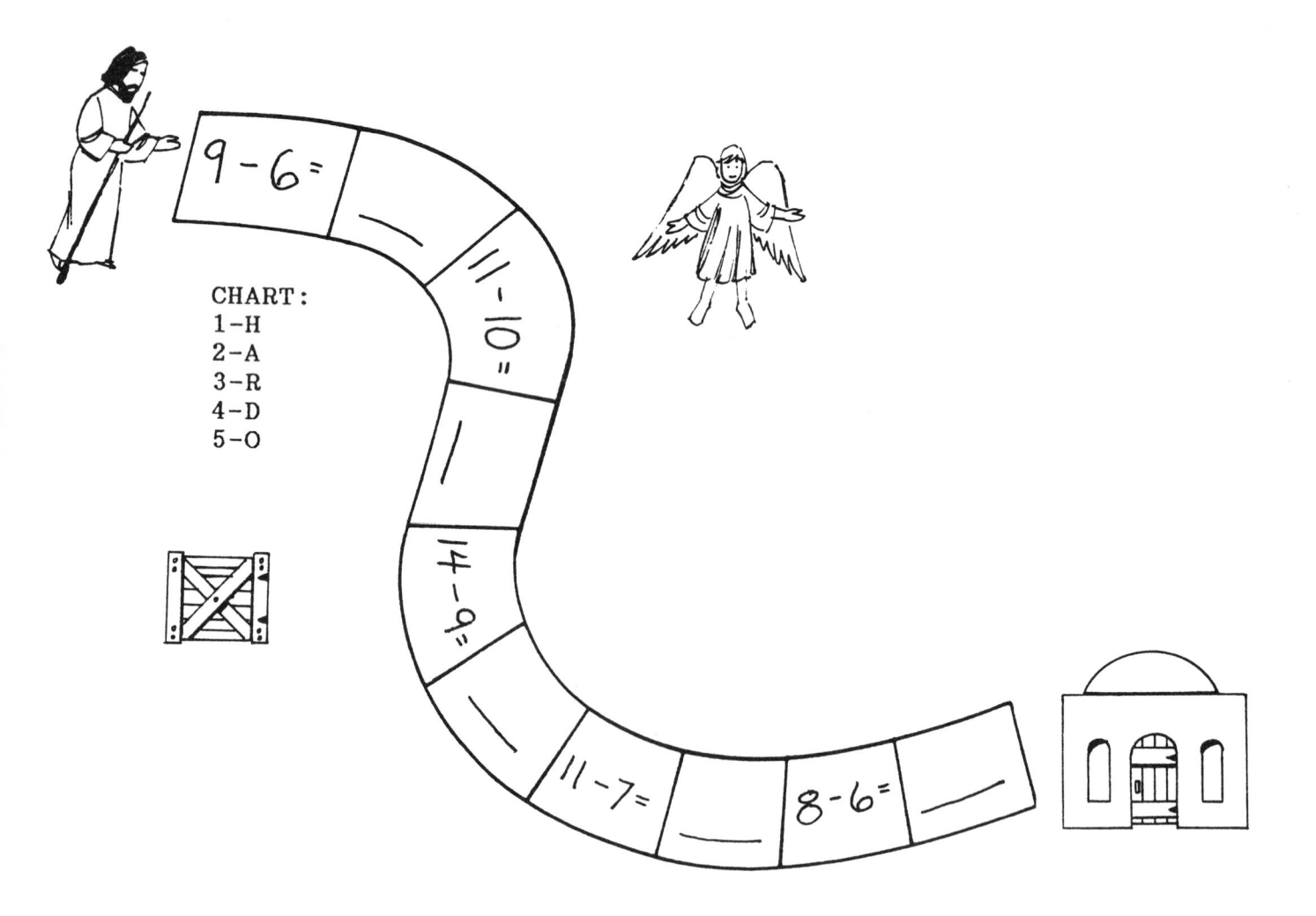

Path squares:
9 - 6 = ___
11 - 10 = ___
14 - 9 = ___
11 - 7 = ___
___
8 - 6 = ___
___

CHART:
1 - H
2 - A
3 - R
4 - D
5 - O

40 © 1993 CPH

THE COLOR PATH

LYDIA AND PAUL
Acts 16:11-15

In the city of Philippi, Paul told a group of women about Jesus. One woman was named Lydia. Lydia's job was to buy and sell beautifully colored fabric. The Lord opened Lydia's heart and she became a believer.

Trace each letter along its path and write it in the circle at the bottom. Some letters will go to a dead end. When you are done, you will see what color of fabric Lydia sold.

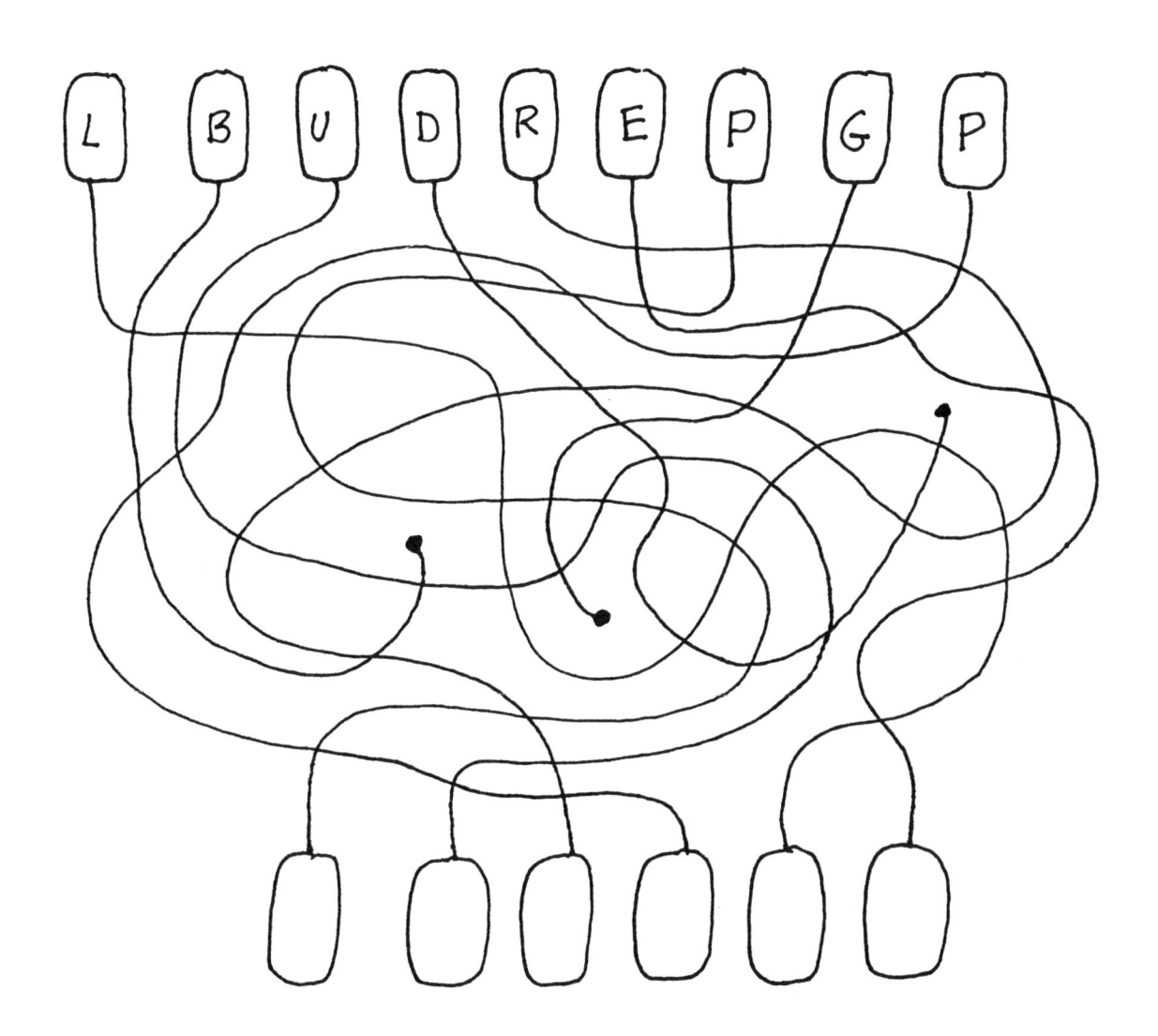

© 1993 CPH

ALL TIED UP   PAUL IMPRISONED IN ROME
                  Acts 28:30-31

Paul was arrested several times for talking about Jesus. Finally he was sent to Rome and imprisoned in a house for two years. God used this difficult time to have Paul do a valuable thing.

Using this code, write the letters on the blanks. You will see the important thing Paul did while he was in this house.

CODE:

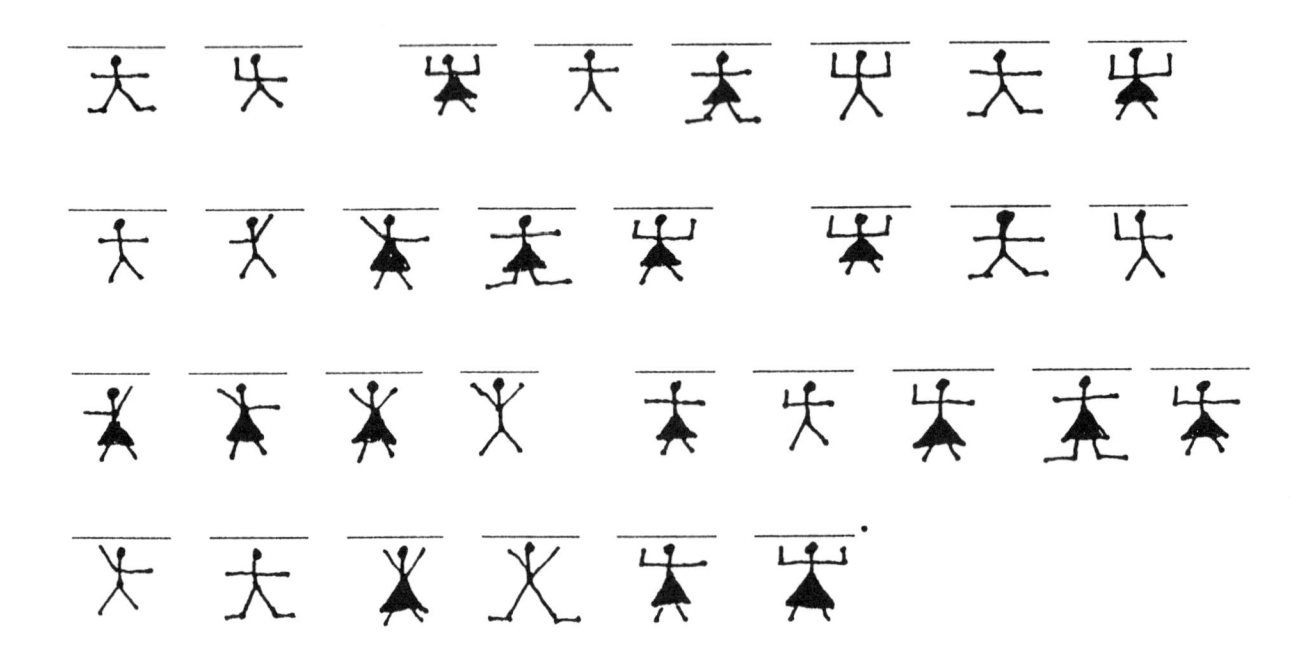

A- E- J- S-
B- G- L- T-
C- H- O- U-
D- I- R-

42 © 1993 CPH

THIS IS IT!   THE LETTER TO THE CORINTHIANS
1 Corinthians 13:13

Paul wrote many letters to new churches. In his first letter to the church at Corinth, he talked about faith, hope, and love. Of these three things, he said that one is the most important. Can you guess which one it is?
Cross out these letters: A, D, J, and N. The remaining letters will spell the correct answer.

A J N D L J D N A O D J A N V D N A J E N D A D J

ALL DRESSED UP   THE ARMOR OF GOD
                       Ephesians 6:11-17

In a letter that Paul wrote to the church at Ephesus, he told them to put on the armor of God. This would help them take a firm stand against the devil.

Draw a line from the word in List 1 to the word that uses matching kinds of letters in List 2. This will show you what each piece of God's armor is made of.

LIST 1   LIST 2

BELT   THE GOSPEL OF PEACE

BREASTPLATE   THE WORD OF GOD

SHOES   OF SALVATION

SHIELD   OF TRUTH

HELMET   OF FAITH

SWORD   OF RIGHTEOUSNESS

44 © 1993 CPH

JUST ASK FOR IT!   THE BOOK OF JAMES
                          James 1:5

James wrote a letter to Christians scattered among different nations. In this letter, he told them an important truth.
Use this code to figure out what James said.

CODE:
A-Z   H-S   O-L   U-F
B-Y   I-R   P-K   V-E
C-X   J-Q   Q-J   W-D
D-W   K-P   R-I   X-C
E-V   L-O   S-H   Y-B
F-U   M-N   T-G   Z-A
G-T   N-M

$\overline{R}\ \overline{U}\quad \overline{Z}\ \overline{M}\ \overline{B}\quad \overline{L}\ \overline{U}\quad \overline{B}\ \overline{L}\ \overline{F}$

$\overline{O}\ \overline{Z}\ \overline{X}\ \overline{P}\ \overline{H}\quad \overline{D}\ \overline{R}\ \overline{H}\ \overline{W}\ \overline{L}\ \overline{N}$,

$\overline{S}\ \overline{V}\quad \overline{H}\ \overline{S}\ \overline{L}\ \overline{F}\ \overline{O}\ \overline{W}$

$\overline{Z}\ \overline{H}\ \overline{P}\quad \overline{T}\ \overline{L}\ \overline{W}$. (James 1:5 NIV)

© 1993 CPH   45

THE GLOWING MAN

JOHN AT PATMOS
Revelation 1:12-16

John was imprisoned on an island called Patmos because he taught people about Jesus. One day while he was worshipping, he had a vision. He heard a voice and saw someone like a son of man. It was Jesus. Read the following verses where John describes what Jesus looked like. Try to find the underlined words in the word search below.

I saw someone "dressed in a <u>robe</u> reaching down to his <u>feet</u> and with a golden <u>sash</u> around his chest. His head and <u>hair</u> were white like <u>wool</u>, as white as <u>snow</u>, and his eyes were like blazing <u>fire</u>. His feet were like <u>bronze</u> glowing in a furnace, and his <u>voice</u> was like the sound of rushing waters. In his right <u>hand</u> he held seven <u>stars</u>, and out of his <u>mouth</u> came a sharp double-edged <u>sword</u>. His face was like the <u>sun</u> shining in all its brilliance."
(Rev. 1:13-16 NIV)

```
D S E B O R B Q B G
V T S R A T S R R K
O D E T Y L X U O U
I R H E O P H A N D
C O C O F O A V Z W
E W W N A F I R E J
I S S A S H R M E L
S N O W H T U O M F
```

HOW MANY CHURCHES?   JOHN WRITES THE BOOK OF REVELATION
Revelation 1:4

When John was on the island of Patmos, God told him to send a message to some churches. John wrote down the message. Today we call this writing the book of Revelation.

Starting at the arrow, figure out the answers to the math problems. Write the last answer in the blank below:

John wrote this message to the _____ churches in the province of Asia.

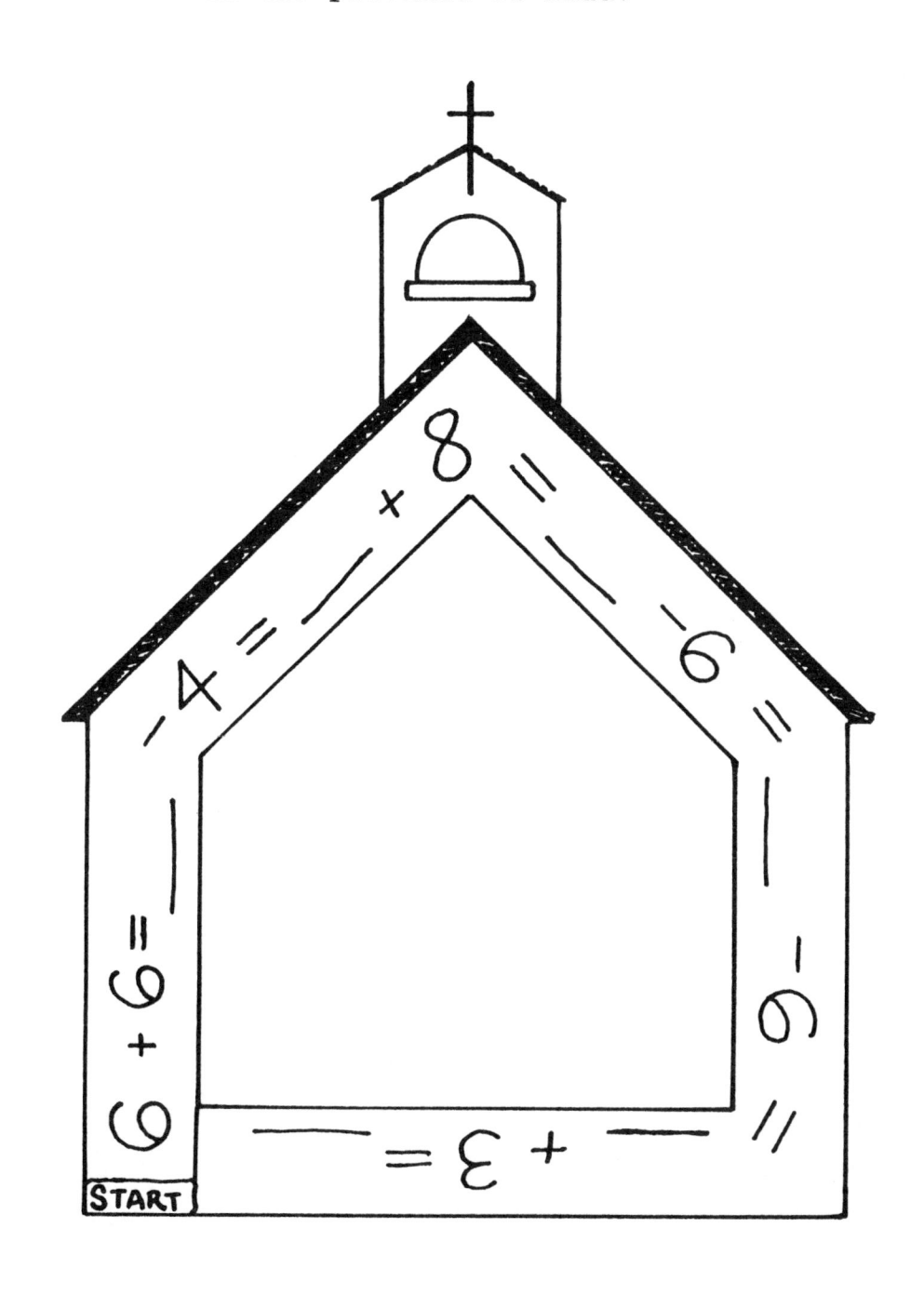

6 + 9 = _ − 4 = _ + 8 = _ − 6 = _ − 1 = _ + 3 = _

START

ANSWERS

A BABY ANNOUNCEMENT

FALLING STARS

LOST AND FOUND

Start

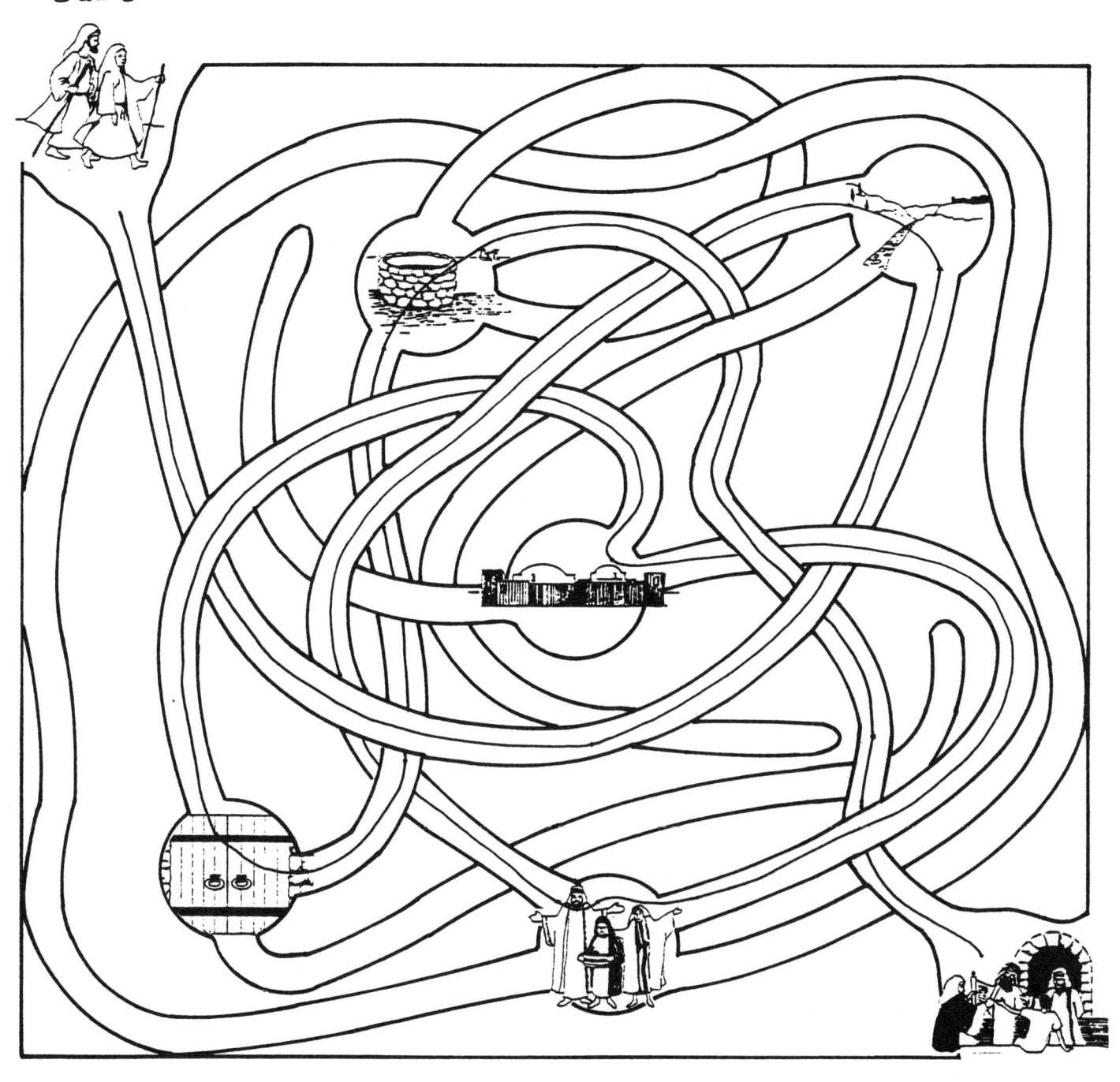

TIME TO GET WET

FOR

FORGIVENESS

OF THEIR

SINS

DID YOU HEAR THAT?

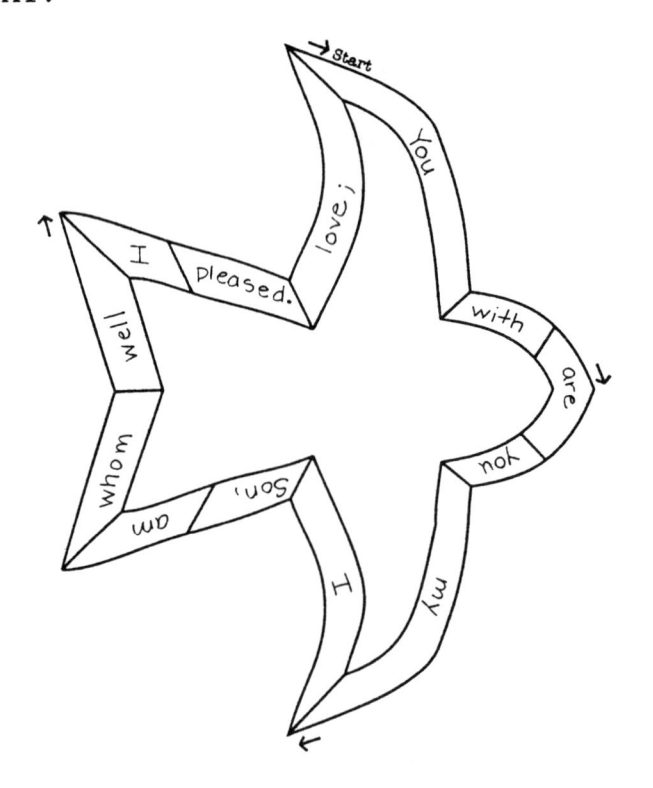

You are my Son, whom I love; with you I am well pleased.

(Luke 3:22 NIV)

A TEMPTING TIME

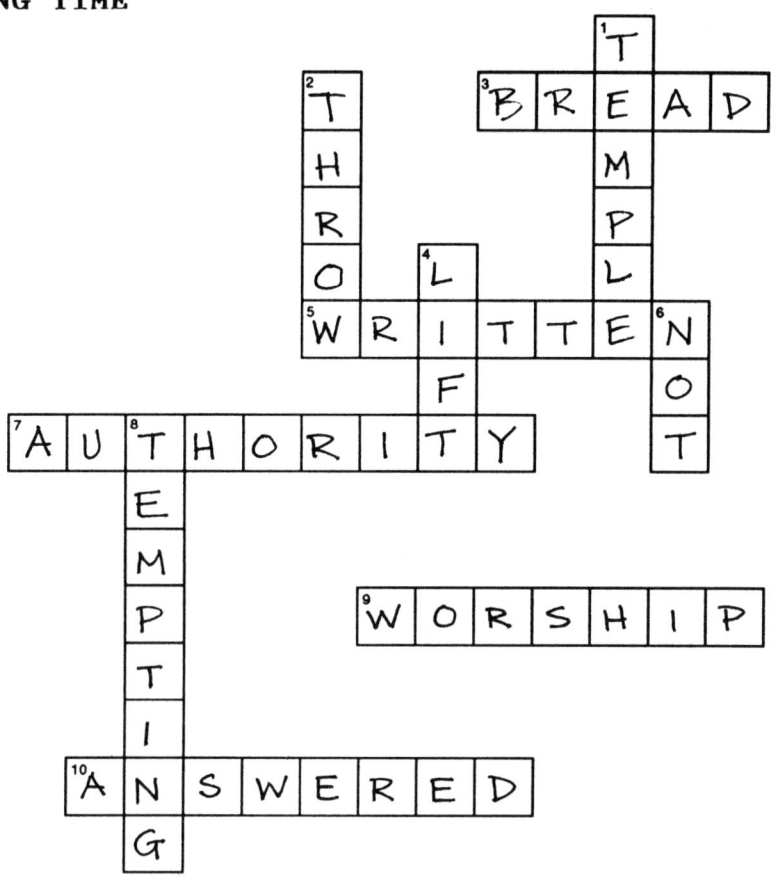

```
            T
         B  R  E  A  D
      T     M
      H     P
      R     L
      O  L  E
   W  R  I  T  T  E  N
         F        O
   A  U  T  H  O  R  I  T  Y
      E
      M
      P        W  O  R  S  H  I  P
      T
      I
   A  N  S  W  E  R  E  D
      G
```

GONE FISHING

ALONE

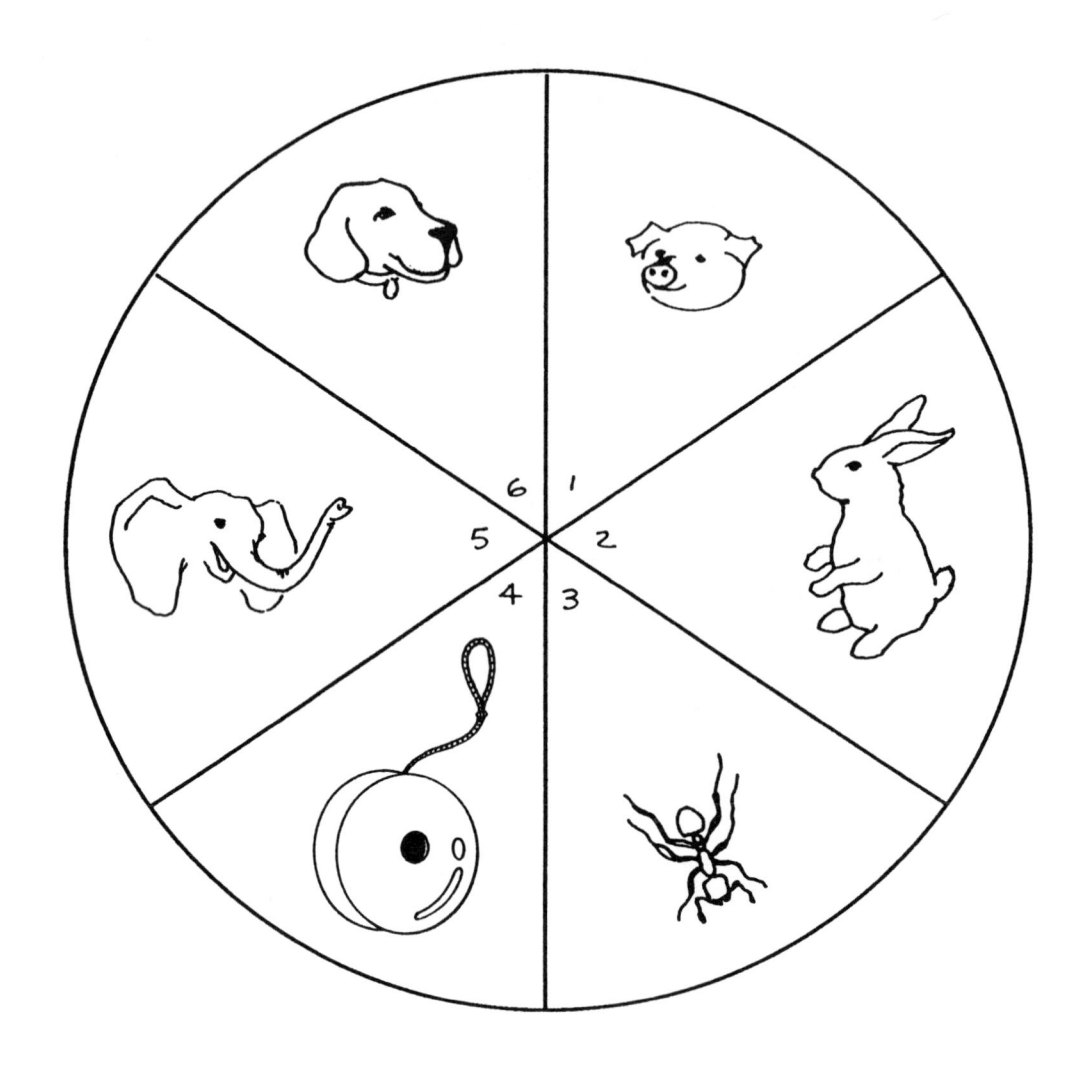

Jesus $\underset{1}{P} \underset{2}{R} \underset{3}{A} \underset{4}{Y} \underset{5}{E} \underset{6}{D}$.

HEAL ME!

H
E
W
E
N
T
D
O
W
N
T
H
R
O
U
G
H
T
H
E
R
O
O
F

He went down through the roof.

A PARTY

$\underset{\triangle 2}{I} \underset{\bigcirc 1}{T} \quad \underset{\triangle 2}{I} \underset{\square 3}{S} \quad \underset{\bigcirc 5}{N} \underset{\diamond 4}{O} \underset{\square 4}{T} \quad \underset{\bigcirc 1}{T} \underset{\triangle 3}{H} \underset{\diamond 2}{E}$

$\underset{\square 1}{H} \underset{\diamond 2}{E} \underset{\bigcirc 3}{A} \underset{\triangle 4}{L} \underset{\bigcirc 1}{T} \underset{\triangle 3}{H} \underset{\diamond 1}{Y} \quad \underset{\bigcirc 2}{W} \underset{\triangle 3}{H} \underset{\diamond 4}{O}$

$\underset{\bigcirc 5}{N} \underset{\square 5}{E} \underset{\diamond 2}{E} \underset{\diamond 3}{D} \quad \underset{\bigcirc 3}{A} \quad \underset{\diamond 3}{D} \underset{\diamond 4}{O} \underset{\triangle 5}{C} \underset{\square 4}{T} \underset{\diamond 4}{O} \underset{\triangle 1}{R},$

$\underset{\bigcirc 4}{B} \underset{\square 2}{U} \underset{\bigcirc 1}{T} \quad \underset{\square 4}{T} \underset{\triangle 3}{H} \underset{\square 5}{E} \quad \underset{\square 3}{S} \underset{\triangle 2}{I} \underset{\triangle 5}{C} \underset{\diamond 5}{K}.$

(Luke 5:31 NIV)

© 1993 CPH

PICK A NUMBER

Start

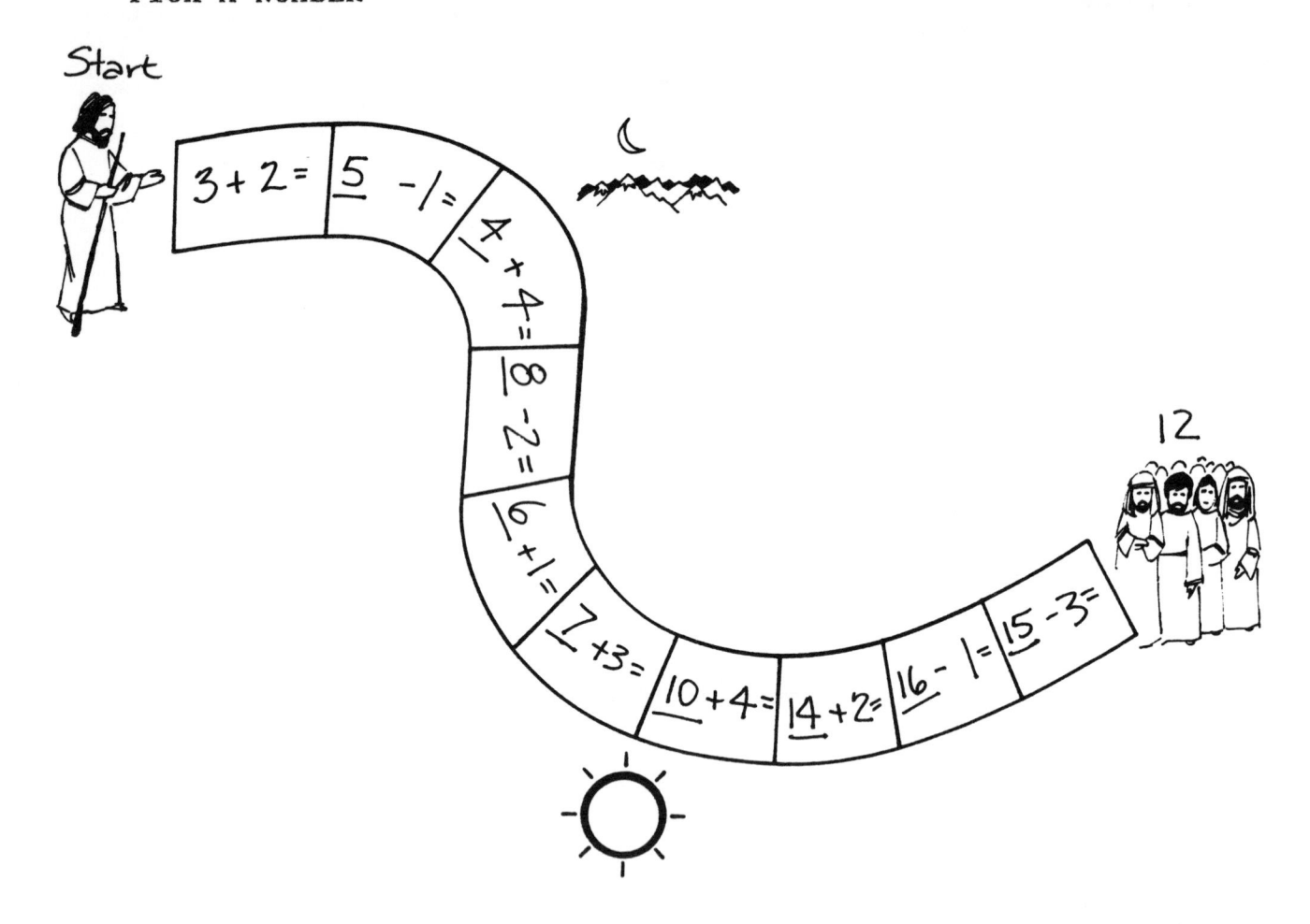

3 + 2 = 5   -1 =
4 + 4 =
8 - 2 =
6 + 1 =
7 + 3 =   10 + 4 =   14 + 2 =   16 - 1 =   15 - 3 =

12

ENEMIES!

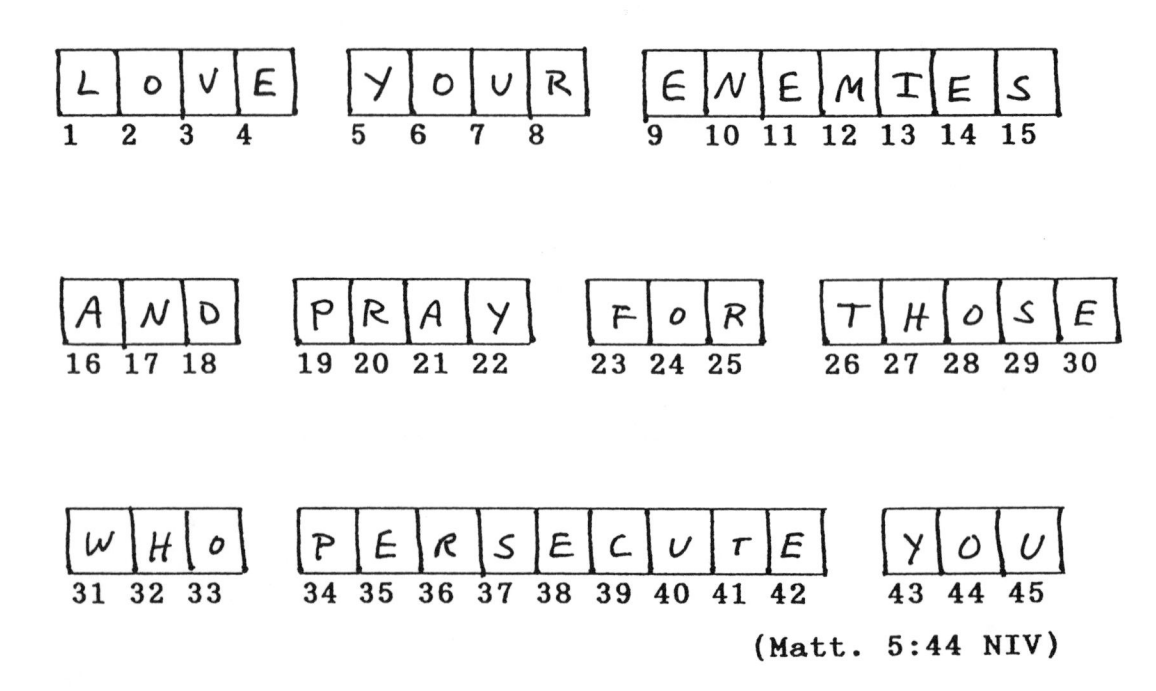

| L | O | V | E | | Y | O | U | R | | E | N | E | M | I | E | S |
| 1 | 2 | 3 | 4 | | 5 | 6 | 7 | 8 | | 9 | 10| 11| 12| 13| 14| 15|

| A | N | D | | P | R | A | Y | | F | O | R | | T | H | O | S | E |
| 16| 17| 18| | 19| 20| 21| 22| | 23| 24| 25| | 26| 27| 28| 29| 30|

| W | H | O | | P | E | R | S | E | C | U | T | E | | Y | O | U |
| 31| 32| 33| | 34| 35| 36| 37| 38| 39| 40| 41| 42| | 43| 44| 45|

(Matt. 5:44 NIV)

56 © 1993 CPH

SPECIAL LOVE

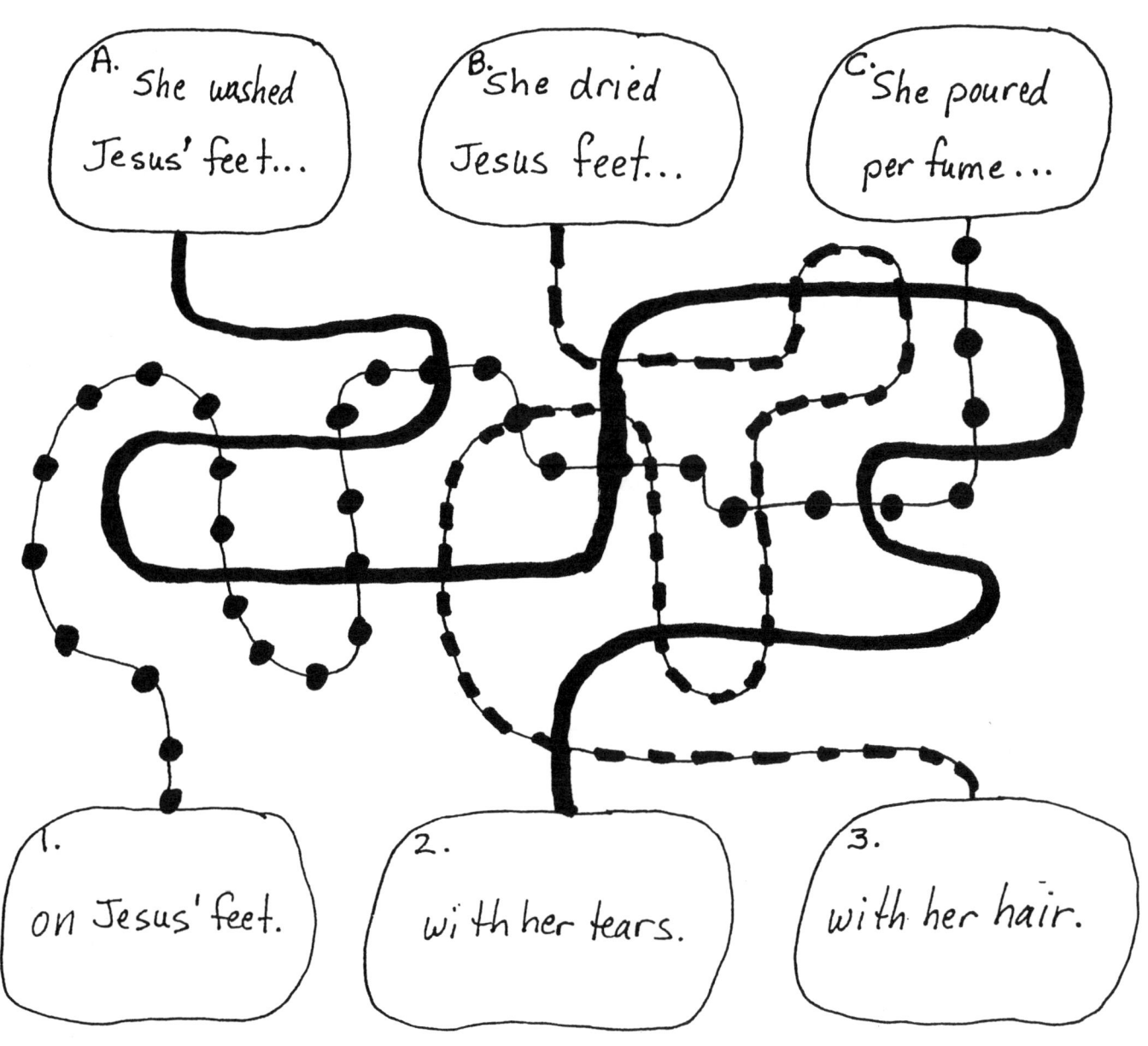

A. She washed Jesus' feet...
B. She dried Jesus feet...
C. She poured perfume...

1. on Jesus' feet.
2. with her tears.
3. with her hair.

A--2
   She washed Jesus' feet with her tears.

B--3
   She dried Jesus' feet with her hair.

C--1
   She poured perfume on Jesus' feet.

© 1993 CPH

STORY TIME

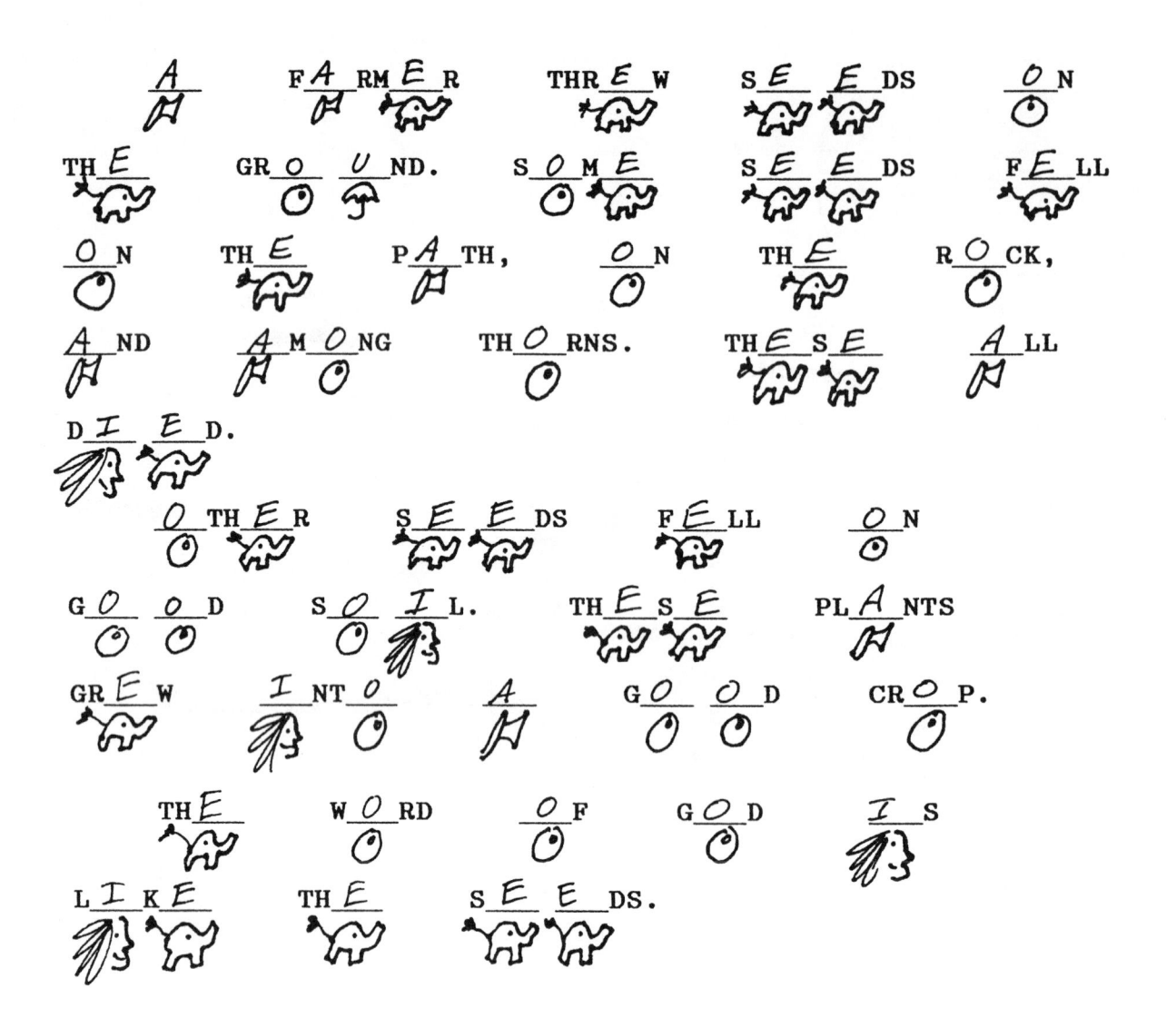

A FARMER THREW SEEDS ON THE GROUND. SOME SEEDS FELL ON THE PATH, ON THE ROCK, AND AMONG THORNS. THESE ALL DIED.

OTHER SEEDS FELL ON GOOD SOIL. THESE PLANTS GREW INTO A GOOD CROP.

THE WORD OF GOD IS LIKE THE SEEDS.

STORMY WEATHER

1 T	2 H	3 E	4 ▓	5 S	6 T	7 O	8 R	9 M	10 ▓
11 ▓	12 ▓	13 S	14 T	15 O	16 P	17 P	18 E	19 D	20 ▓
21 ▓	22 A	23 N	24 D	25 ▓	26 ▓	27 ▓	28 T	29 H	30 E
31 ▓	32 ▓	33 ▓	34 W	35 A	36 T	37 E	38 R	39 ▓	40 ▓
41 G	42 R	43 E	44 W	45 ▓	46 ▓	47 C	48 A	49 L	50 M.

DON'T PACK A SUITCASE

Take nothing for the journey—
no staff, no bag, no bread,
no money, no extra tunic.

(Luke 9:3 NIV)

WE'RE HUNGRY!

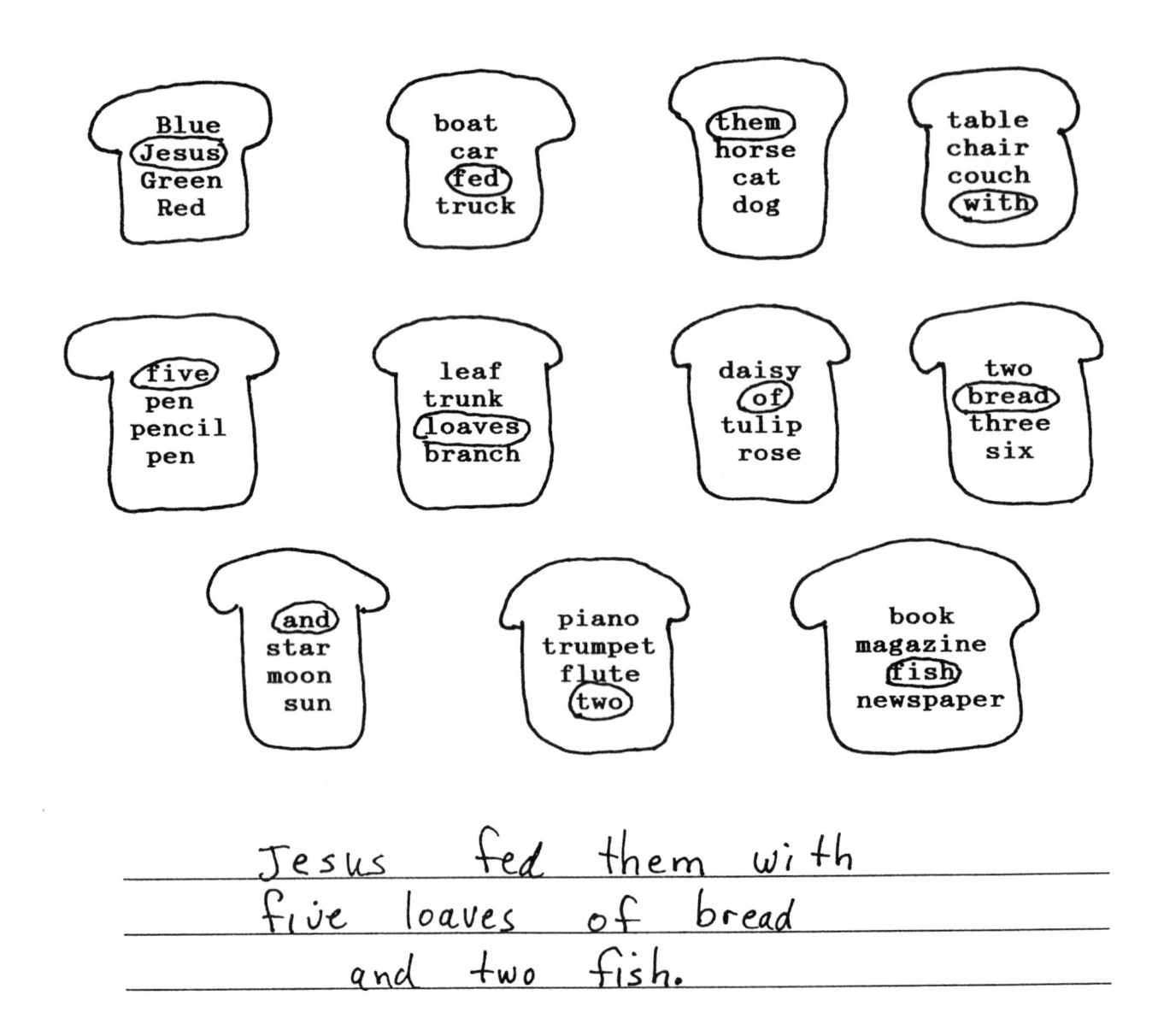

Bread 1: Blue, (Jesus), Green, Red
Bread 2: boat, car, (fed), truck
Bread 3: (them), horse, cat, dog
Bread 4: table, chair, couch, (with)
Bread 5: (five), pen, pencil, pen
Bread 6: leaf, trunk, (loaves), branch
Bread 7: daisy, (of), tulip, rose
Bread 8: two, (bread), three, six
Bread 9: (and), star, moon, sun
Bread 10: piano, trumpet, flute, (two)
Bread 11: book, magazine, (fish), newspaper

Jesus fed them with five loaves of bread and two fish.

WHO AM I?

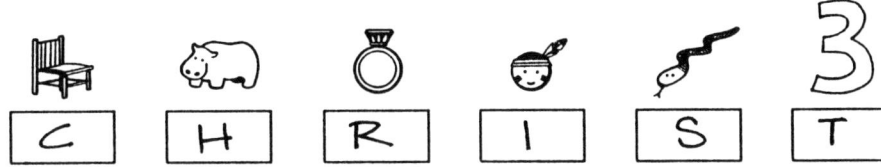

T H E

C H R I S T

O F

G O D

THE VOICE

T H I S   I S   M Y   S O N,

W H O M   I   H A V E

C H O S E N;   L I S T E N

T O   H I M. (Luke 9:35 NIV)

© 1993 CPH

ROAD SIGNS

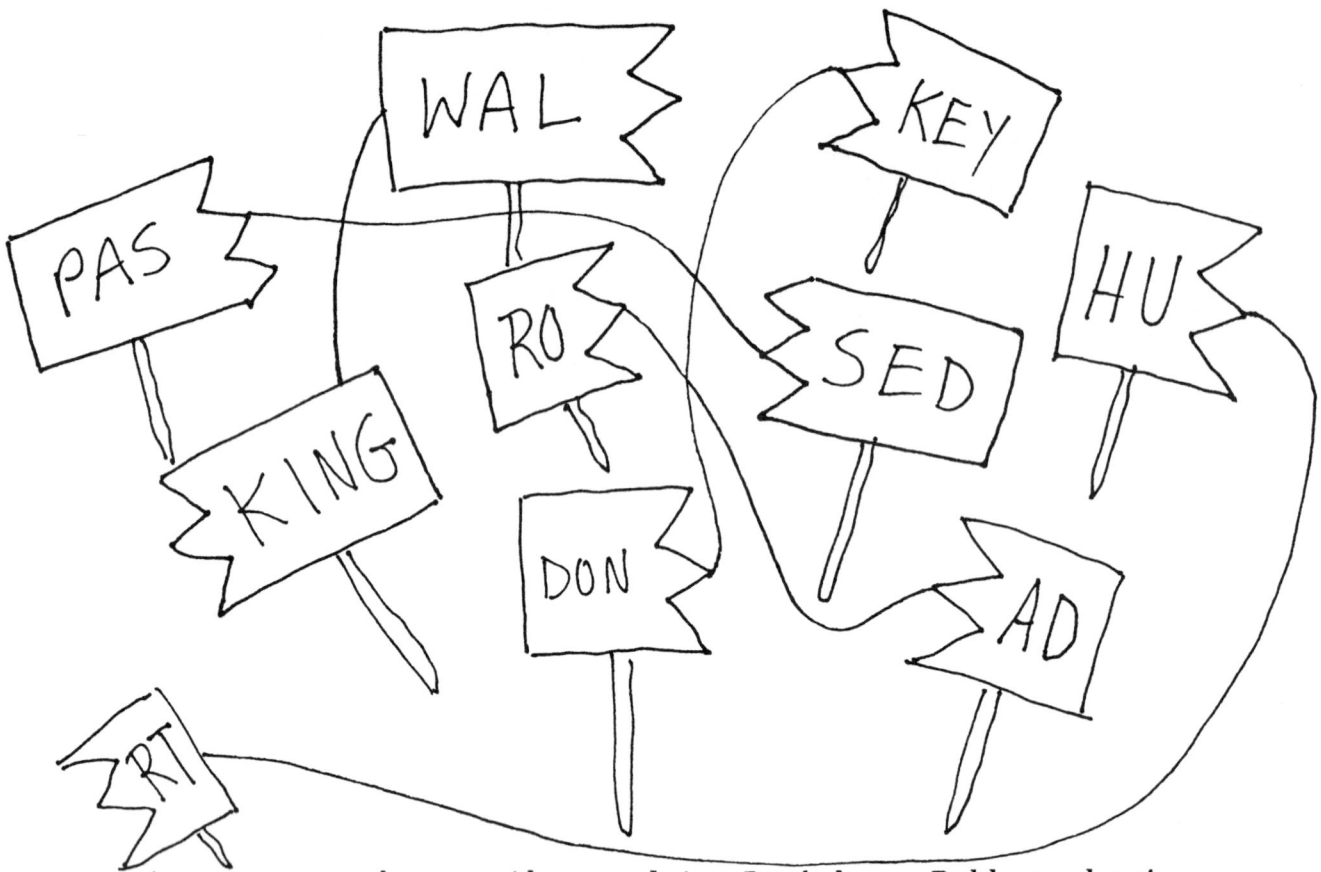

A man was going on the road to Jericho. Robbers beat him and left him lying in the ROAD. A priest came WALKING down the road. When he saw the hurt man, he passed by on the other side of the road. A Levite came along the road. He PASSED by on the other side, too. A Samaritan also came along. When he saw the HURT man, he stopped and helped him. He put the man on his DONKEY and took him to an inn until he got well.

HOW?

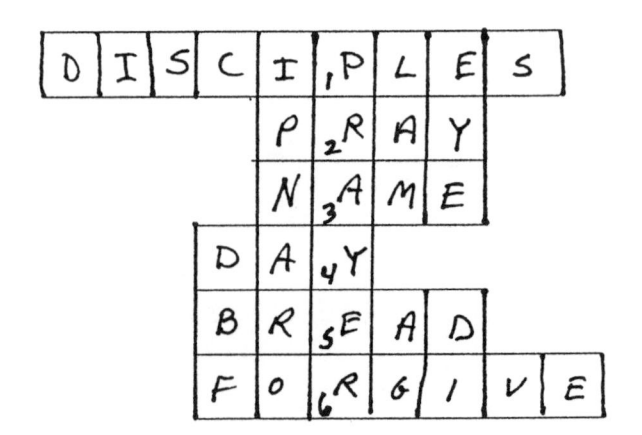

$\frac{P}{1}\ \frac{R}{2}\ \frac{A}{3}\ \frac{Y}{4}\ \frac{E}{5}\ \frac{R}{6}$

D	I	S	C	I	P	L	E	S
					R			
				P	R	A	Y	
				N	A	M	E	
			D	A	Y			
			B	R	E	A	D	
			F	O	R	G	I	V	E

© 1993 CPH

I FOUND IT!

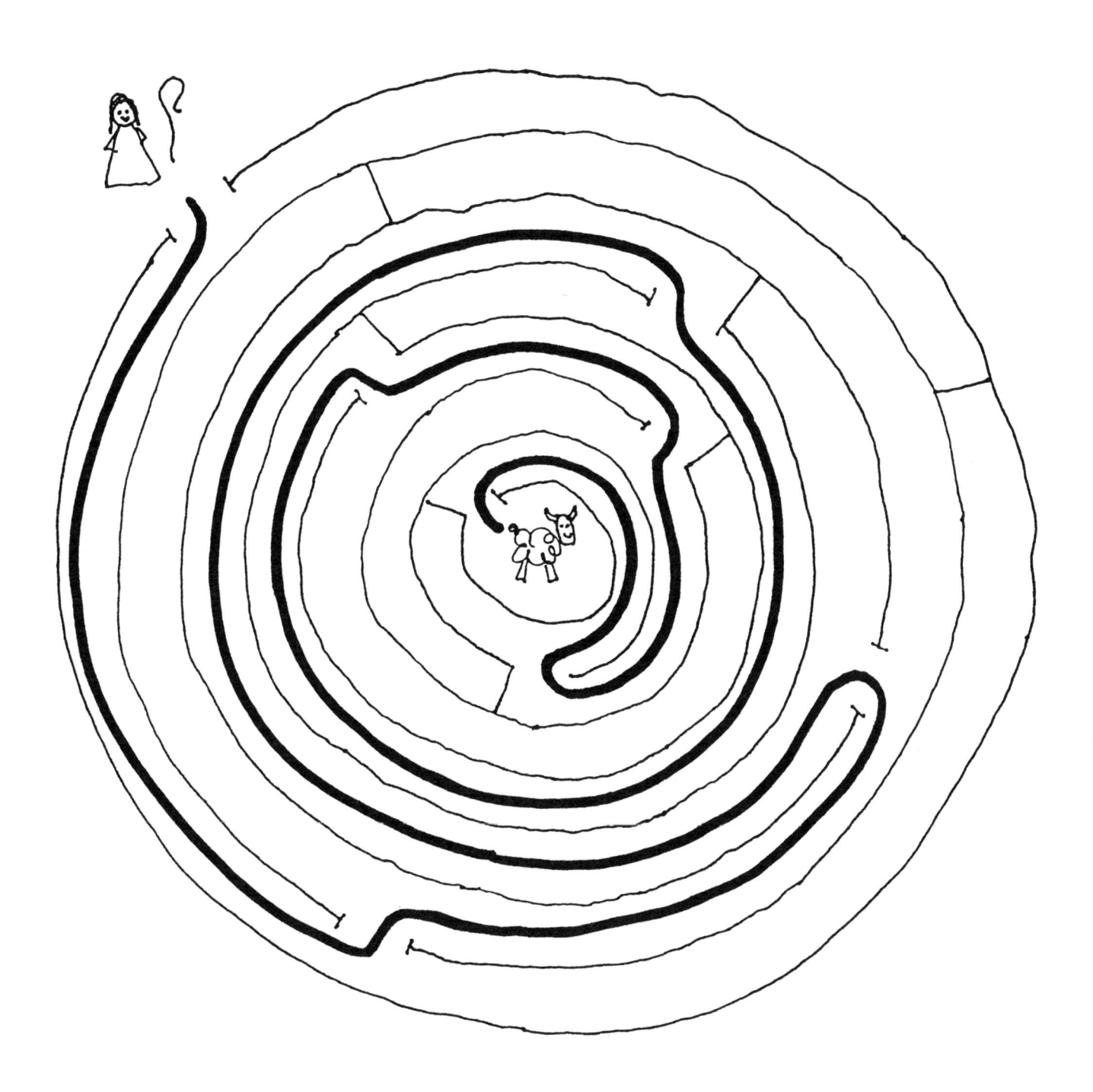

HOME AGAIN

My son was lost
but now is found.

GO AWAY?

$\underset{10}{J}\ \underset{5}{E}\ \underset{19}{S}\ \underset{21}{U}\ \underset{19}{S}\quad \underset{19}{S}\ \underset{1}{A}\ \underset{9}{I}\ \underset{4}{D},$

"$\underset{12}{L}\ \underset{5}{E}\ \underset{20}{T}\quad \underset{20}{T}\ \underset{8}{H}\ \underset{5}{E}\quad \underset{12}{L}\ \underset{9}{I}\ \underset{20}{T}\ \underset{20}{T}\ \underset{12}{L}\ \underset{5}{E}$

$\underset{3}{C}\ \underset{8}{H}\ \underset{9}{I}\ \underset{12}{L}\ \underset{4}{D}\ \underset{18}{R}\ \underset{5}{E}\ \underset{14}{N}\quad \underset{3}{C}\ \underset{15}{O}\ \underset{13}{M}\ \underset{5}{E}$

$\underset{20}{T}\ \underset{15}{O}\quad \underset{13}{M}\ \underset{5}{E}.$" (Matt. 19:14 NIV)

64 © 1993 CPH

COME DOWN, ZACCHAEUS!

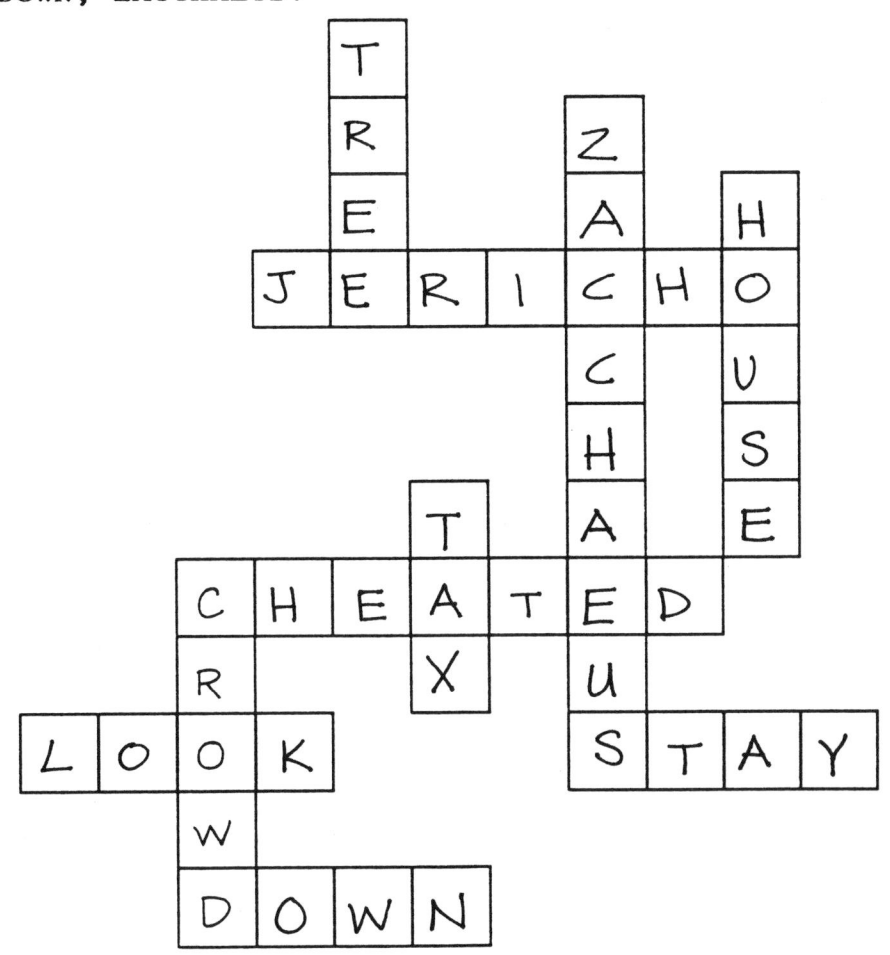

Crossword answers:
- TREE
- JERICHO
- ZACCHAEUS
- HOUSE
- CHEATED
- TAX
- CROW(N) / CROWD
- LOOK
- STAY
- DOWN

PRAISE THE LORD!

HOSANNA! BLESSED

IS HE WHO COMES

IN THE NAME

OF THE LORD!

(John 12:13 NIV)

A FINAL MEAL

1. THE

2. LAST

3. SUPPER

THE KISS

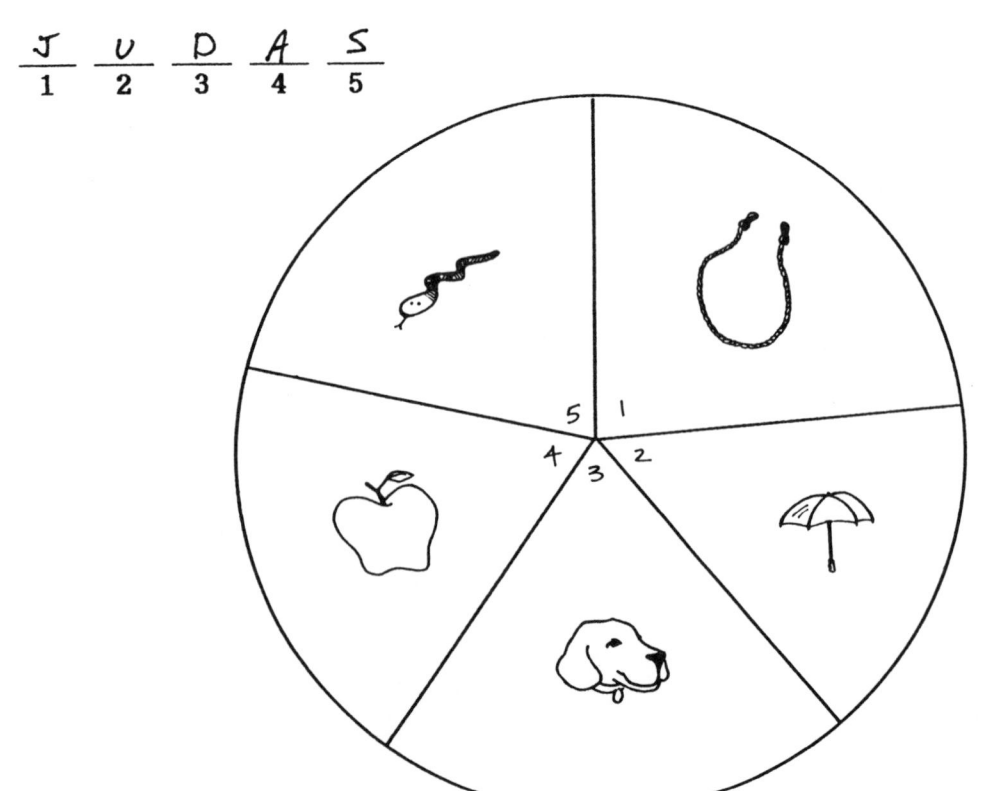

$\frac{J}{1} \frac{U}{2} \frac{D}{3} \frac{A}{4} \frac{S}{5}$

TRUE LOVE

F A T H E R, F O R G I V E T H E M,
1 2 3 4 5 6 7 8 9 10 11 12 13 14 15 16 17

F O R T H E Y D O N O T K N O W
18 19 20 21 22 23 24 25 26 27 28 29 30 31 32 33

W H A T T H E Y A R E D O I N G.
34 35 36 37 38 39 40 41 42 43 44 45 46 47 48 49

(Luke 23:34 NIV)

WHERE IS HE?

Why do you look for the living among the dead? He is not here; he has risen!

(Luke 24:5-6 NIV)

© 1993 CPH

I DOUBT IT!

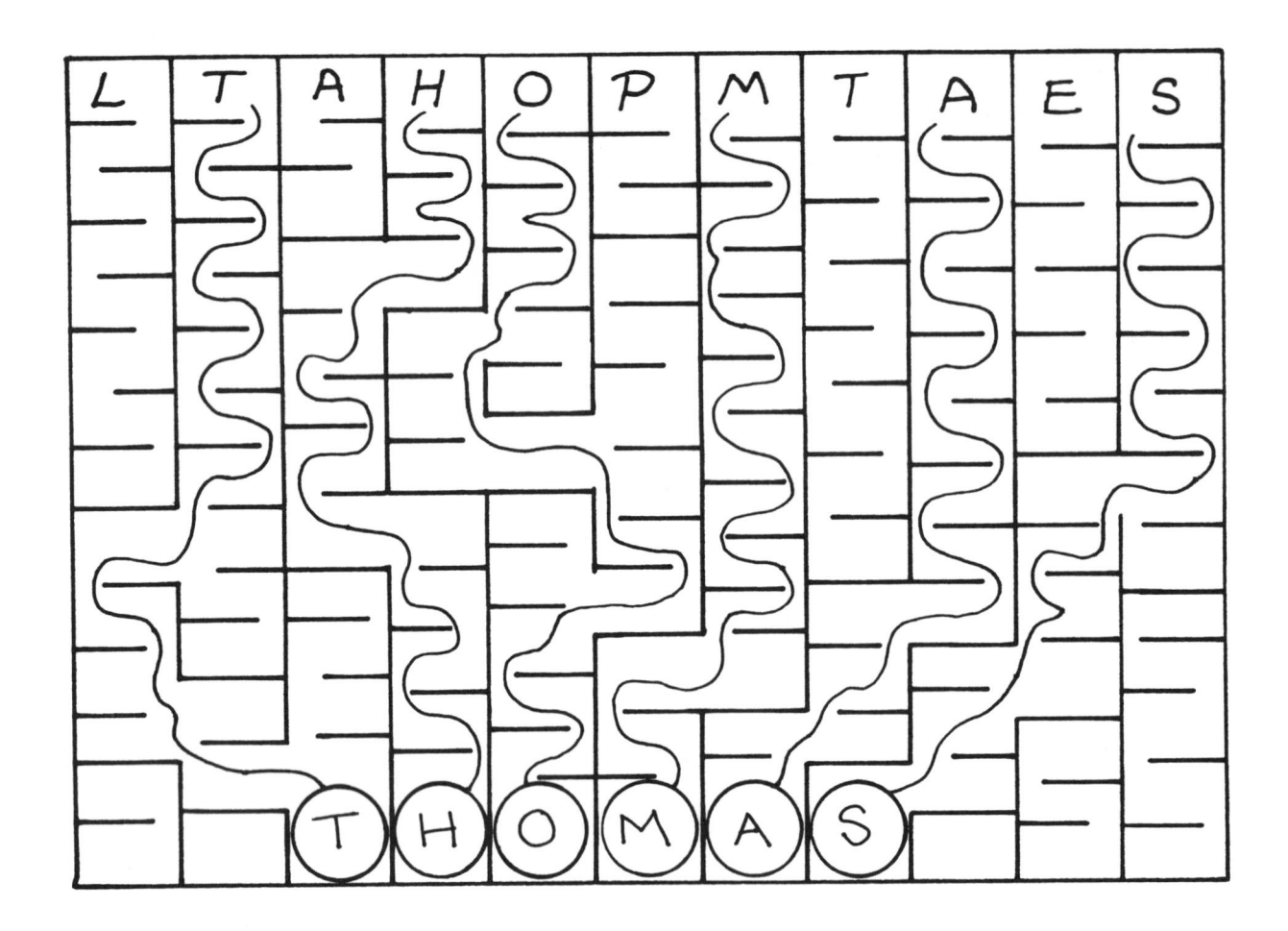

THOMAS

UP, UP, AND AWAY

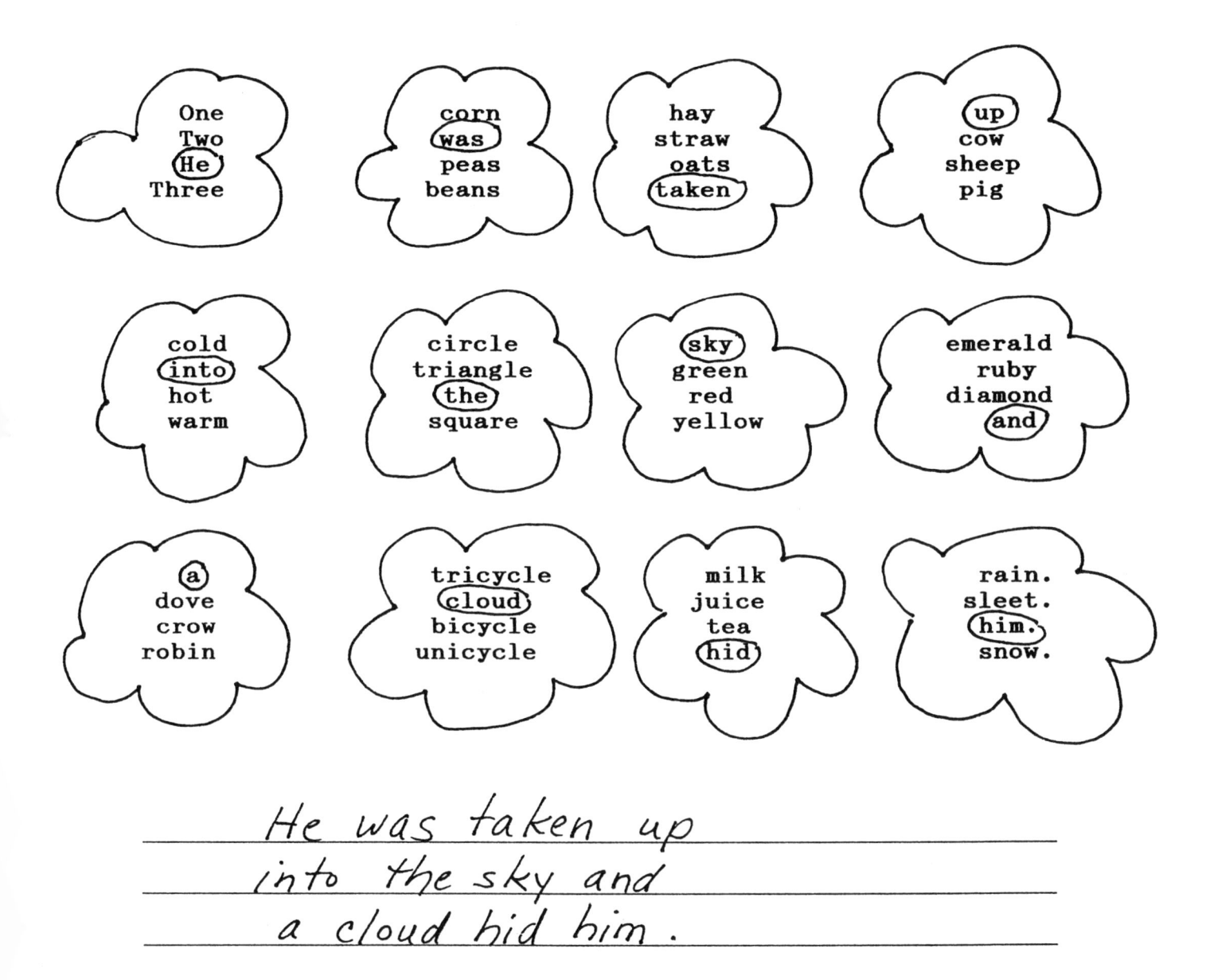

- One / Two / **(He)** / Three
- corn / **(was)** / peas / beans
- hay / straw / oats / **(taken)**
- **(up)** / cow / sheep / pig
- cold / **(into)** / hot / warm
- circle / triangle / **(the)** / square
- **(sky)** / green / red / yellow
- emerald / ruby / diamond / **(and)**
- **(a)** / dove / crow / robin
- tricycle / **(cloud)** / bicycle / unicycle
- milk / juice / tea / **(hid)**
- rain. / sleet. / **(him.)** / snow.

He was taken up
into the sky and
a cloud hid him.

A WONDERFUL, WONDER-FILLED DAY

ALL OF THEM WERE FILLED WITH THE HOLY SPIRIT AND SPOKE IN OTHER LANGUAGES.

WALK!

ONE DAY, PETER AND JOHN WERE GOING TO THE TEMPLE. A CRIPPLED MAN STOPPED THEM AND ASKED FOR MONEY. PETER SAID, "SILVER OR GOLD I DO NOT HAVE, BUT WHAT I HAVE I GIVE YOU. IN THE NAME OF JESUS, WALK!" THE MAN JUMPED TO HIS FEET AND BEGAN TO WALK! HE PRAISED GOD FOR THIS MIRACLE.

THIS NEWS IS GOOD NEWS

		³P	⁴H	⁵I	⁶L	⁷I	⁸P		
¹¹T	¹²O	¹³L	¹⁴D			¹⁷H	¹⁸I	¹⁹M	
		²³T	²⁴H	²⁵E		²⁷G	²⁸O	²⁹O	³⁰D
	³²N	³³E	³⁴W	³⁵S					
			⁴⁴A	⁴⁵B	⁴⁶O	⁴⁷U	⁴⁸T		
	⁵²J	⁵³E	⁵⁴S	⁵⁵U	⁵⁶S				

WHO TURNED ON THE LIGHT?

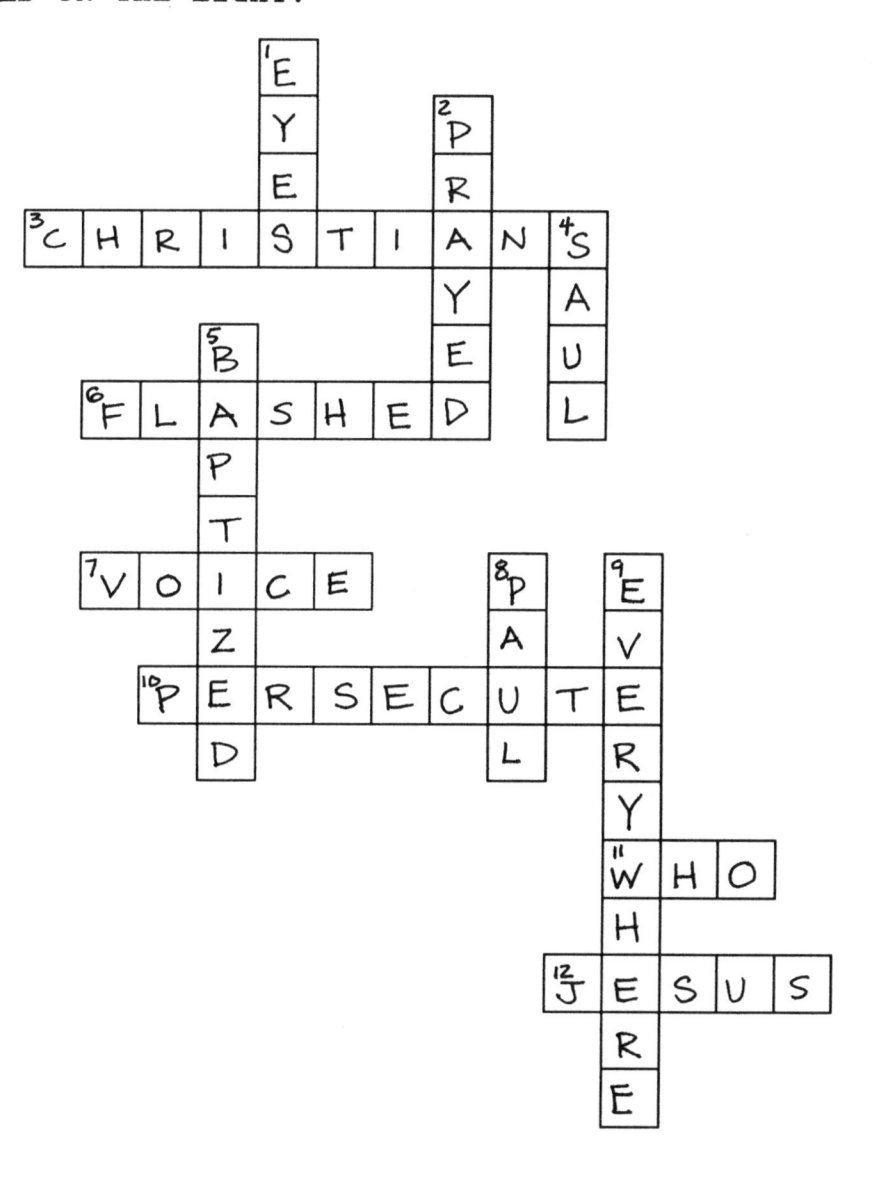

Across:
3. CHRISTIAN
6. FLASHED
7. VOICE
10. PERSECUTE
11. WHO
12. JESUS

Down:
1. EYE
2. PRAYE (PRAYED)
4. SAUL
5. BAPTIZED
8. PAUL
9. EVERYWHERE

© 1993 CPH

71

WHAT'S FOR DINNER?

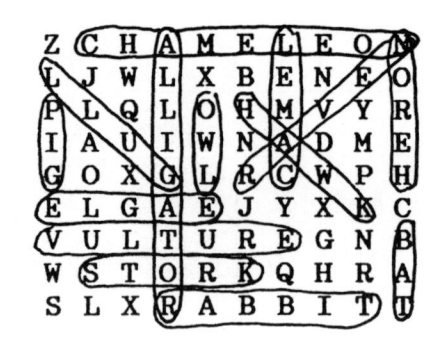

```
Z C H A M E L E O N
L J W L X B E N F O
P L Q O H M V Y R E
I A U I W N A D M H
G O X G L R C W P H
E L G A E J Y X K C
V U L T U R E G N B
W S T O R K Q H R A
S L X R A B B I T T
```

KNOCK, KNOCK, WHO'S THERE?

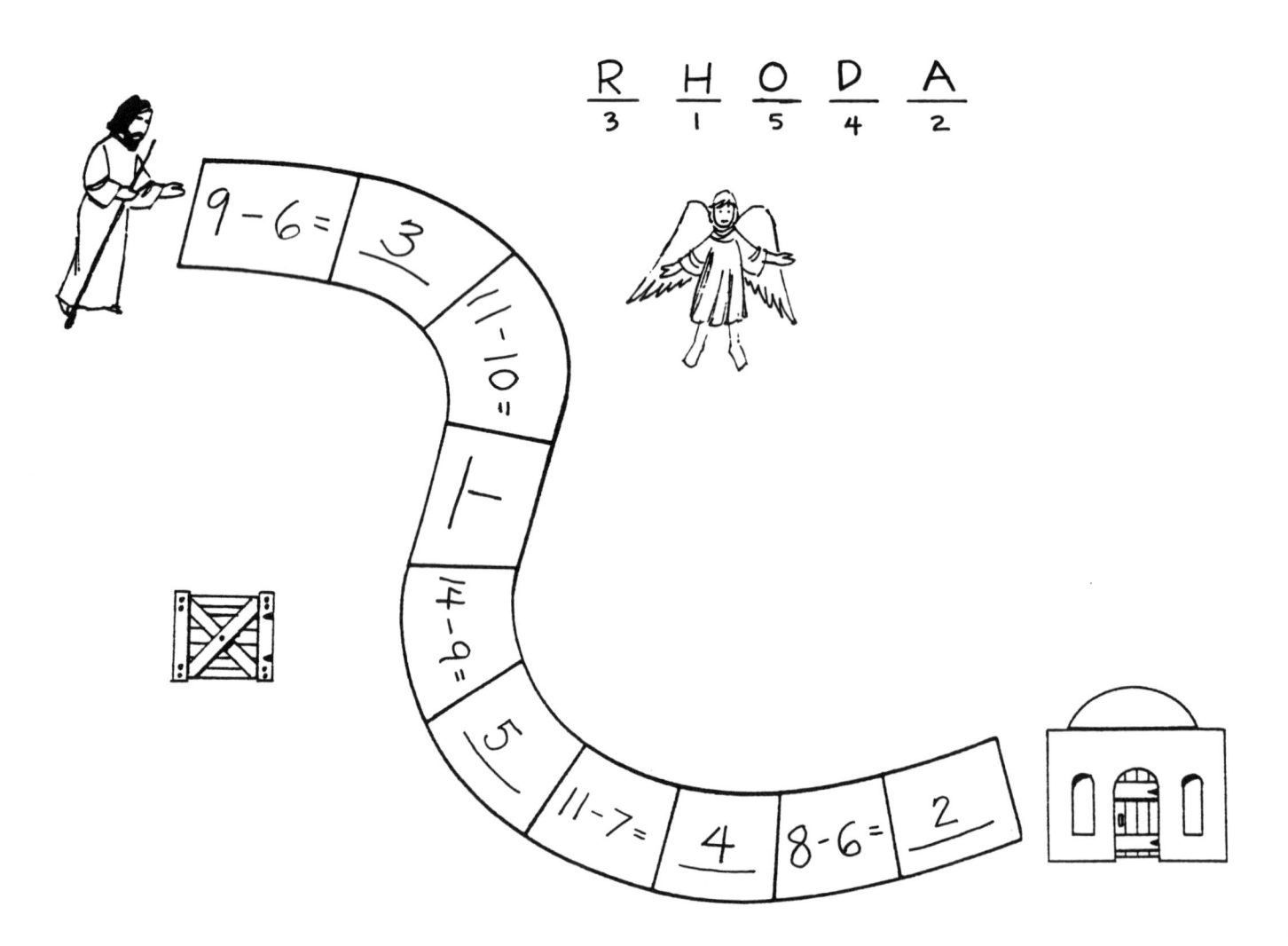

$\underset{3}{R} \underset{1}{H} \underset{5}{O} \underset{4}{D} \underset{2}{A}$

9 − 6 = 3
11 − 10 = 1
14 − 9 = 5
11 − 7 = 4
8 − 6 = 2

THE COLOR PATH

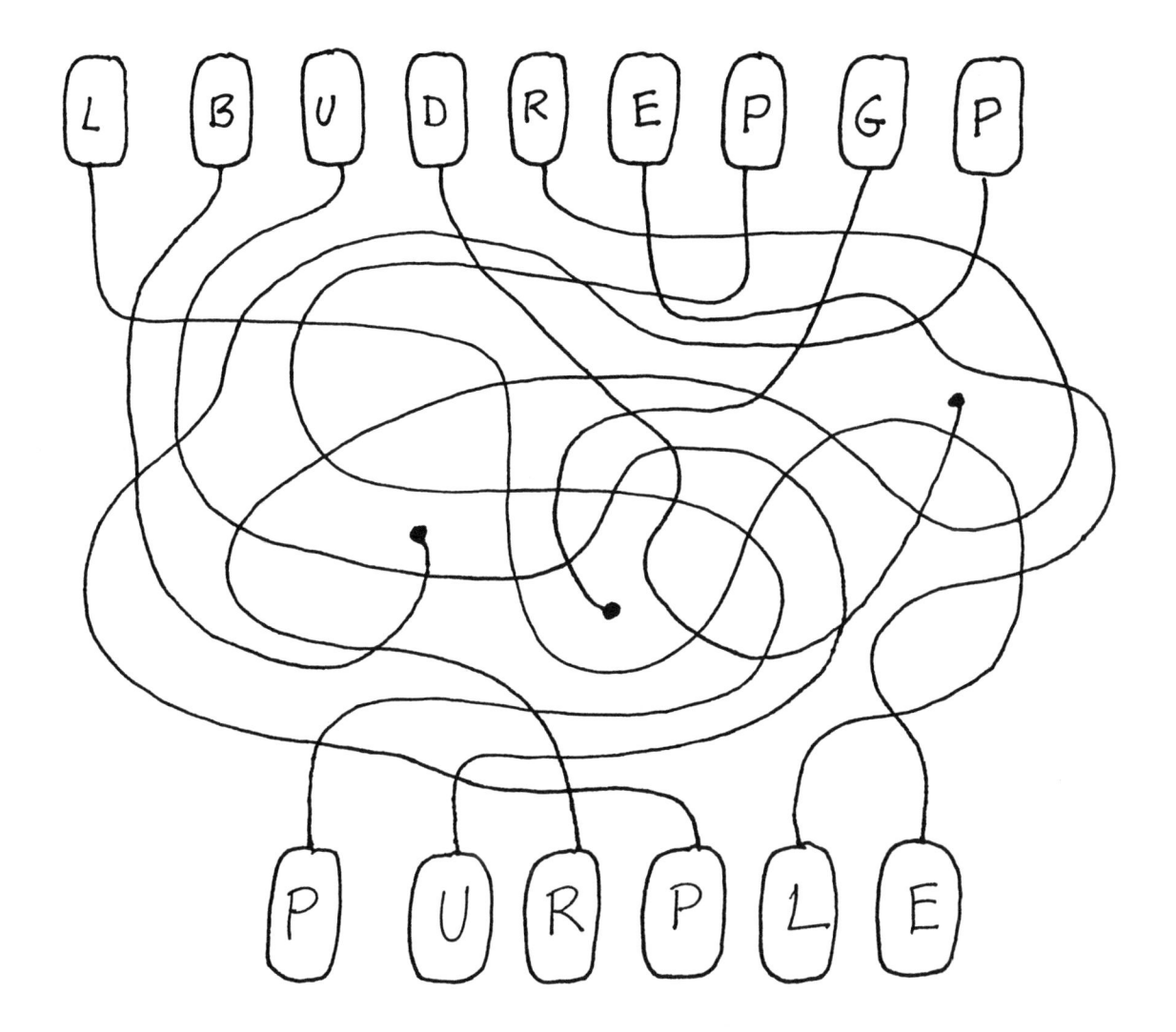

ALL TIED UP

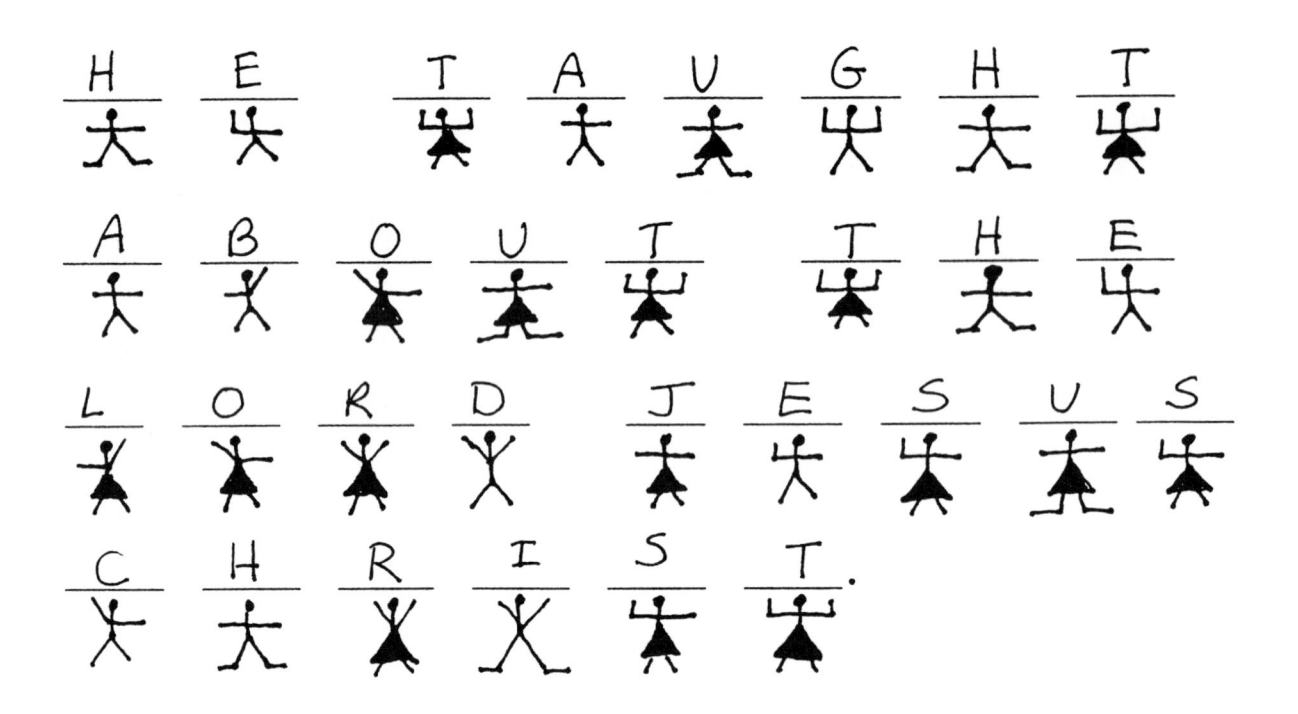

HE TAUGHT
ABOUT THE
LORD JESUS
CHRIST.

THIS IS IT!

LOVE

ALL DRESSED UP

LIST 1	LIST 2
BELT	THE GOSPEL OF PEACE
BREASTPLATE	THE WORD OF GOD
SHOES	OF SALVATION
SHIELD	OF TRUTH
HELMET	OF FAITH
SWORD	OF RIGHTEOUSNESS

© 1993 CPH

JUST ASK FOR IT!

$\underset{R}{I} \underset{U}{F} \quad \underset{Z}{A} \underset{M}{N} \underset{B}{Y} \quad \underset{L}{O} \underset{U}{F} \quad \underset{B}{Y} \underset{L}{O} \underset{F}{U}$

$\underset{O}{L} \underset{Z}{A} \underset{X}{C} \underset{P}{K} \underset{H}{S} \quad \underset{D}{W} \underset{R}{I} \underset{H}{S} \underset{W}{D} \underset{L}{O} \underset{N}{M},$

$\underset{S}{H} \underset{V}{E} \quad \underset{H}{S} \underset{S}{H} \underset{L}{O} \underset{F}{U} \underset{O}{L} \underset{W}{D}$

$\underset{Z}{A} \underset{H}{S} \underset{P}{K} \quad \underset{T}{G} \underset{L}{O} \underset{W}{D}.$ (James 1:5 NIV)

THE GLOWING MAN

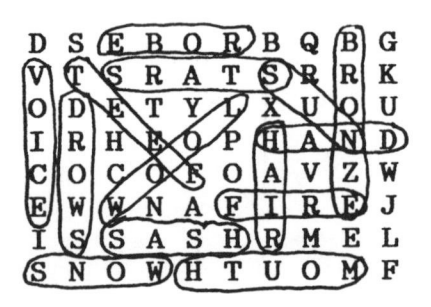

76   © 1993 CPH

HOW MANY CHURCHES?

John wrote this message to the __7__ churches in the province of Asia.

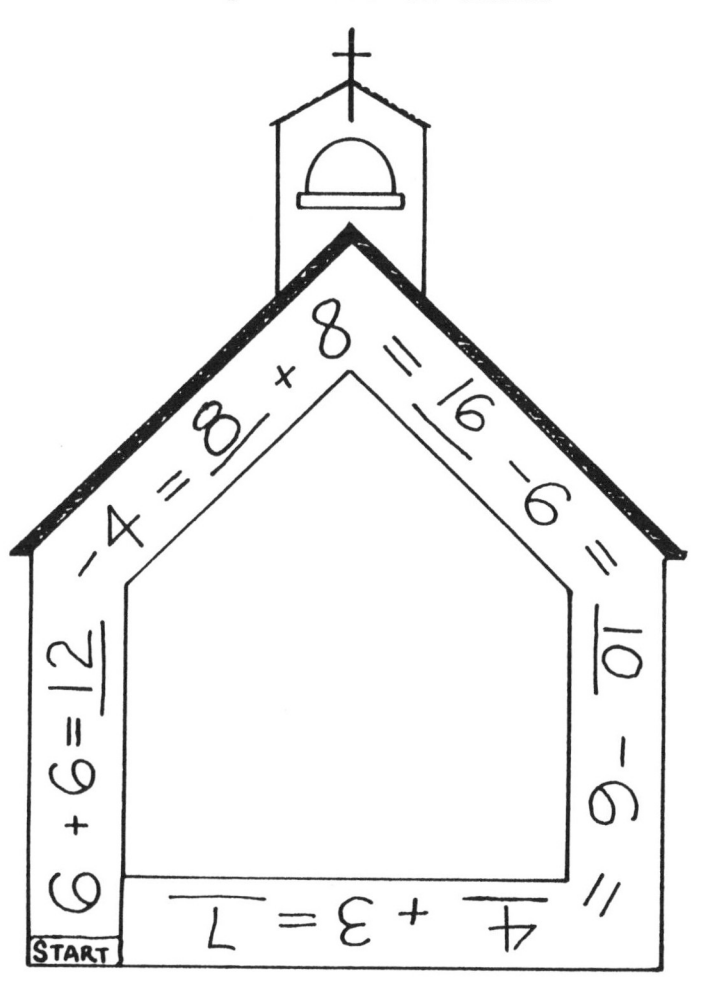

6 + 6 = 12
-4 = 8 + 8 = 16
-6 = 10
-9 = 1
4 + 3 = 7

START